Blogging and Other Social Media

Blogging and Other Social Media

Exploiting the Technology and Protecting the Enterprise

ALEX NEWSON

WITH DERYCK HOUGHTON

AND JUSTIN PATTEN

Routledge
Taylor & Francis Group

LONDON AND NEW YORK

First published 2009 by Gower Publishing

2 Park Square, Milton Park, Abingdon, Oxon OX14 4RN
711 Third Avenue, New York, NY 10017, USA

Routledge is an imprint of the Taylor & Francis Group, an informa business

First issued in paperback 2016

British Library Cataloguing in Publication Data
Blogging and other social media : exploiting the technology and protecting the enterprise
  1. Social media 2. Business enterprises - Computer network resources 3. Blogs 4. User-generated content
  5. Internet marketing
  I. Newson, Alex II. Houghton, Deryck III. Patten, Justin
  658'.054678

  ISBN 978-0-566-08789-9 (hbk)
  ISBN 978-1-138-25547-0 (pbk)

Library of Congress Cataloging-in-Publication Data
Newson, Alex.
  Blogging and other social media : exploiting the technology and protecting the enterprise / by Alex
  Newson, with Deryck Houghton and Justin Patten.
    p. cm.
  Includes bibliographical references and index.
  ISBN 978-0-566-08789-9
  1. Business communication--Blogs. 2. Blogs. 3. Social media. 4. Business enterprises--Blogs. I.
  Houghton, Deryck. II. Patten, Justin. III. Title.
  HD30.37.N49 2008
  659.20285'4678--dc22

                                                                                    2008028243

Contents

List of Figures

How to Use this Book

This book is aimed at both organizations that already use social media, and those considering the matter for the first time. It is not only a practical guide to using the different forms of media; it also acts as a guide to the wider issues such as and considers social media from a number of perspectives.

For those unfamiliar with social media, we recommend starting from the beginning and working your way through Parts 1 and 2. These two parts should not be ignored even if you already use social media, we hope that they help you get even more out of the exciting new types of participation that the internet has on offer.

If you are thinking about using a particular form of social media (for example, wikis), again go straight to the relevant part of either chapter in Parts 1 or 2. For those considering using social media within their organization, for example, to collect know-how or assist with a project, go to Part 3.

The final part is a guide to the risks associated with social media. Chapter 18 gives an overview of the law. Chapter 19 looks at managing online reputation.

Foreword

The web is fundamentally about people – though it wasn't really seen like that until comparatively recently. The worldwide web was and is a web of 'sites', and the current transformation that is convulsing both the worldwide web and the markets that rely on and feed off it is, perhaps, in economic terms a 'correction' that is pushing it into being a web of people who use sites as communication nodes to communicate with other people. In that sense, 'Web 2.0' is taking the topology of the internet and mapping it to the social world we want to live in.

This probably needs explaining further. The ad hoc interconnectedness of the internet is being increasingly mirrored in the social relationships and enablers for those relationships as they exist online. In other words, the medium is now heavily influencing the messages, methods and modes of communication we use to interact with each other. This is arguably the nature of the Web 2.0 'revolution', which is, of course, not a revolution at all: now that the infrastructure is in place for mass collaboration, it must happen.

The reason Web 2.0 is not a revolution is that it was bound to happen. It was the next logical step for the actors to take. The web is a stage on which new kinds of online lives are being acted out. Without people, it would have no reason to exist. Without people to use, explore and expand it, it would not be expanding. So the web is fundamentally about people, but now the infrastructure increasingly allows us to create the 'value' that can be exploited for corporate gain.

The possibility of value that is created by the users themselves, rather than by the creators of the sites they interact on, is an irresistible idea. Web 2.0 sites represent, in a sense, the very essence of the 'build it, and they will come' idea of the web. They represent the previous Net generation's urge to make information free, separating corporate messages from what people really want to do online – talk to each other. But, of course, Web 2.0 also represents a potentially limitless free ride – sites whose content creates itself. Who needs journalists when bloggers do it for free? Who needs consumer experts when real, live consumers can tell each other what their experiences were really like? Any company that can work out how to make money from creating the 'room' in which a community can interact and play most likely doesn't need to create very much content for that community. Build it, and they will come. This isn't to say building it is easy – the various travails that have troubled Facebook over what to make available and how good are examples of the privacy and commercial challenges such companies face. This also isn't to say that blogging will make journalists redundant, or that online grassroots consumer action will remove the need for meaning – quite the opposite, I would say.

The reality is, of course, that we are truly working for the corporate world – sites are made and we put the content on them, we make them popular, we provide advertiser information, and all for no salary. Before, we interacted with websites in a more lop-sided way; we consumed information and advertising on the side, or shopped in places that made our lives easier. In essence, something was offered out for consumption and we either consumed it or we didn't. This mode of online life is still huge, and while high-street retailers' bricks and mortar stores can carry on selling DVDs and CDs for hard cash, it will remain in its growth phase – when the users of the web realize they are paying for all that mall space and those staff salaries and not for the content, the drive to take it all online will be only briefly halted by the hopeless pleas of telecoms firms struggling to cope with the load. Perhaps the work of the record companies and their law firms might hold it up a bit, too. But the initial online world of 'more of the same, just online' is being radically redrawn.

Journalists know this well. If at any point in reading this book you wondered why you should take advice as a business on social media and related topics from lawyers, rather than, say, web-heads, it might help to remember that the online world is a world of communication. Journalists have always relied on one or more people in the background in publishing businesses who can tell you whether what you're doing is going to cost you a small fortune – or possibly send you to jail. Journalists rarely embark on a career in the press without legal training, for very good reasons. This doesn't mean they stay out of trouble all the time – all decisions to publish are based on degrees of legal risk, and the only safe magazine, newspaper or website is one filled with blank pages.

It is this last point that I feel makes a bunch of lawyers worth listening to when it comes to the advantages and pitfalls of Web 2.0 and beyond. People like me listen to them all the time. We don't always do as they say, but we know why they say it. The only really safe way to engage with this brave new online conversational world is not to engage with it at all.

Lawyers are experienced professionals in the art of communication, like journalists, PR people and marketers. The areas covered in this book span the current world of social media, and as I've pointed out the world of social media is one of communications. Brand value and product saleability could hinge on what companies do in the social media areas their consumers inhabit, and will certainly hinge on what their consumers say about them. Marketing and advertising companies are learning those lessons and the tools to leverage the power of 'the wisdom of crowds' – such as it is. But when the word on the street is negative, the liberating nature of the internet means companies may also have little to no realizable right of redress with those saying damaging things about them – take-downs can take ages (though often they are straightforward) and the words on a blog today can do enormous damage to a company, with the unhappy complement that the value of suing a blogger for libel is most likely nil. Even bringing the libel suit could cost you even more brand damage. David and Goliath comparisons have rarely been more aptly made.

This is not all about blogs. In fact, Web 2.0 (or 3.0) probably will not be 'about blogs' in a few years at all. Blogs to me are one of the symptoms of a society that is rapidly and often blindly metamorphosing into the Information Society. Will millions of Africans take to blogging as Africa is wirelessly connected? Will the Chinese blog their way into their future as the next world superpower? Possibly – but consider this: ten years ago, no one used Google – now the company rules the internet. Five years ago YouTube didn't exist. Two years ago probably no one in the UK had heard of Facebook. Blogging, as words on a web page, may look to the new web users of 2013 as archaic as bulletin boards do to us now.

This is not to say blogs are already 'over' – their usefulness for disseminating information is unarguable. The way they can be used to personalize corporations and create one-person information businesses is a modern marvel. But in the same way that most people online have graduated straight to video, as it were, Web 2.5 bloggers may be very different animals from today's web writers.

The enormous upside for businesses of the social media 'revolution' is that it should let businesses talk more openly and constructively both within themselves and with their customers. The need for, and some of the results of, the so-called 'Web 2.0 revolution' were in fact presaged at least as far back as 1999, if not well before, by various people, including the a group of web activists who wrote down their thoughts as the Cluetrain Manifesto. Let's not forget that in 1999 most people had barely started to use Google. I mention Cluetrain because it holds some of the key lessons companies that want to swim in the fascinating waters of Web 2.0 and beyond need to learn. They stem from the basis that, as I have said, the web is all about people.

It is not necessary to read the Cluetrain book to get the essence of what was being said in 1999 – just the opening paragraphs on their website will do:

> A powerful global conversation has begun. Through the Internet, people are discovering and inventing new ways to share relevant knowledge with blinding speed. As a direct result, markets are getting smarter – and getting smarter faster than most companies.
>
> These markets are conversations. Their members communicate in language that is natural, open, honest, direct, funny and often shocking. Whether explaining or complaining, joking or serious, the human voice is unmistakably genuine. It can't be faked.
>
> Most corporations, on the other hand, only know how to talk in the soothing, humorless monotone of the mission statement, marketing brochure, and your-call-is-important-to-us busy signal. Same old tone, same old lies. No wonder networked markets have no respect for companies unable or unwilling to speak as they do.
>
> They will only sound human when they empower real human beings to speak on their behalf.[1]

In a very real sense the Cluetrain manifesto was a call to arms for Web 2.0, and it came true – companies that do not provide a human face in some way generate a reputation for poor customer service that spreads like wildfire and is very hard to correct. From price comparison websites for almost everything you can think of to online social networks discussing anything from the quality of parenting books to what kind of financial advice to take, the global market as an increasingly disintermediated conversation between people is hardly a million miles from the truth already. Just imagine where it will be in five years.

---

1   Chris Locke, Doc Searls, David Weinberger (1999), Manifesto, The Cluetrain website, http://www.cluetrain.com.

One of the things you can say about the world in five years time is that most people aged 35 or under will have never known a time without the web in their adult shopping lives. They will automatically gain referrals and opinions on your firm from online peers, some of whom they will never have met but, nonetheless, whose opinion will be valued far above the view they have of your firm's traditional marketing. It is how they will buy, or at the very least shortlist, everything else, and it would be folly to believe they'd buy your services based on another model.

What Cluetrain was about, if it was about any one thing, was trying to get the corporate world to let its people talk to the people outside. This is now happening in a highly fractured way – from blogs by Microsoft employees to staffers at Web 2.0 companies such as Flickr engaging constantly in online debates with users.

But as companies are gradually pulled into this more personal, and personable, world they will also pull the social media world into themselves. Social media software tools and methods will, I remain convinced, revolutionize the way companies work by allowing effective collaboration and communication across departmental and hierarchical boundaries. Software companies are also convinced of this, and are all, from Google to Microsoft to Adobe to a couple of guys in a garage who no one has yet heard of, developing the next generation of collaborative workflow systems because they know that the workers of the near future will be able to use them in business to make businesses work better.

The proof of all this, at least in very small part, is in your hands – or perhaps on your screen – right now.

There would seem to be several problems associated with having a book about 'social media': first, it's a book, not a website, and as such harks automatically back to 'dead trees', authorial elitism and the Old Guard; second, it will suffer from being out of date almost from the moment it's printed. But, in its defence, this book was produced using an online wiki-style collaborative word-processing environment (Google Docs in this case) by a group of authors in different companies who all have aligned ideas; it could also easily be turned into an online, iterative publication that incorporates work by people outside its author group and includes future chapters on social media currently only being dreamed up in a college dorm room. There is no reason this cannot be done, and I hope that it does happen.

What you are reading is a product of a brave new world of social creativity. The very fact that the sentence 'this book was produced using an online wiki-style collaborative word-processing environment' makes sense, that we know what it means, and that it could not have been written 15 years ago with anything like the same meaning behind it, is a neon signpost pointing us along the road to this new world.

All that's left is for you to work out how to use those tools to enable the conversations that are possible, both within a business, creatively and usefully swapping knowledge and experience, and without, creating interpersonal relationships with future markets. It's about you, and how you do this. Because it's all about people.

Rupert White
Technology Journalist

PART 1
Blogs

Introduction to Blogs CHAPTER

1

Blogs have had a dramatic impact on the internet, whether we're talking about personal or corporate, amateur or professional parts of the net. Whilst we cannot be sure about what the first blog was, or when that blog was created, what we do know is that blogs have been massively popular since at least the year 2000. Writing this book in 2007–08, blogs remain an established part of the internet and do not look to be going away any time soon. In this part of the book, we discuss what blogging is, take a whistlestop tour through some of the main issues the prospective blogger need consider, and give guidance on how to set up and maintain a blog.

Whilst this book is aimed at the business user, many of the suggestions and comments given will be equally useful to those considering setting up a personal blog.

What is a Blog?

Blog is a term derived from 'web log'. A blog is a website where information is displayed in date order, with the most recent information at the top of the page.

The reason for the analogy to a log or journal becomes clear when you browse through a blog; take a look at any of the blogs we mention in this chapter. When you open a blog, as described above, you will see the various entries ordered by date (but with the latest entry first). From the current entry, you can scroll down to read earlier entries. In this way, an actively maintained blog will develop and grow from day to day.

As well as the information being displayed in date order, one thing that all blogs have in common is that the majority, usually all, link to information on other websites. If a statement is made, a blog will typically justify that statement by linking to the source of the information behind the statement.

Authoring a blog, maintaining one or adding an article to an existing blog is called *blogging*. Individual articles on a blog are called *blog posts*, *posts* or *entries*. A person who posts these entries is called a *blogger*.

For those not of an overly technical bent, the blog concept could offer a fairly arid start to this book. To illustrate in more detail just what the concept means in reality, let's examine some categories of blog and then some examples of blogs.

Categories of Blog

Blogs can be categorized in many different ways – most blog directories divide them by subject matter. The categories of blog are incredibly varied; here are some of the main categories:

- academic
- arts
- blogging – how to blog
- business and professional
- entertainment
- financial
- food
- jobs and careers
- technology
- personal
- politics
- sports.

Within these broad categories, there are often hundreds or even thousands of blogs, which can be further categorized. For example, within the business and professional category, there are blogs on every type of business and profession that exists. Taking law blogs as simply one example, these fall into at least three categories:

1. **'Pure law' blogs**: Written by legal academics, the purpose of these blogs is to discuss a particular area or areas of law. Whilst most of the writers of these blogs are university academics, sometimes they are written by professionals from law firms, patent agents or trade mark agents.

2. **Law firm blogs**: Written by a specific law firm, or sometimes a lawyer at a particular law firm, these blogs generally discuss and provide information on legal areas that the law firm practises. These sorts of blogs are usually less 'academic' in feel than the pure law blogs, and discuss wider issues than the law itself. For example, law firm blogs often discuss the work of that firm and commercial subjects.

3. **Personal blogs**: Diaries and commentaries written from a personal perspective by people who happen to be lawyers. Whilst these may touch upon legal subjects, the main focus is on the person and their feelings rather than on the law from an academic or business perspective.

The same is true of many other blogging subject areas; blogs are as diverse as their writers. To get an idea of the spectrum of blogs, take a look at the vast directory on Technorati (http://www.technorati.com).

Examples of Blogs

LIFEHACKER
(http://www.lifehacker.com/)

Lifehacker is a popular US blog that tells you how to 'streamline your life', normally by using technology but sometimes by more 'low-fi' means. In a typical week, Lifehacker will blog on how to use your existing technology more efficiently or better, link to useful new software and websites, and even tell you an easy way to de-seed a watermelon!

The blog is owned and published by Gawker Media, an independent media company that produces a range of blogs. It is written by a small team headed by Gina Trapini. Lifehacker was launched in 2005. We spoke to Trapini, who told us that the blog was inspired by the term 'life hack', coined by tech. journalist Danny O'Brien in 2004. O'Brien did a presentation at O'Reily's ETech conference called 'Life Hacks: Tech Secrets of Overprolific Alpha Geeks.' You can see more about it at http://en.wikipedia.org/wiki/Life_hack

Lifehacker is funded by the advertising that is featured on the blog.

Since its launch, Lifehacker has rapidly risen to be one of the most popular blogs. It has received many awards, including being rated by *Time* magazine as one of the 50 coolest websites of 2005 and winning 'Best Group Blog' in the Weblog Awards 2007.

Like a number of successful blogs, the writings of the Lifehacker team have turned up in a more traditional form of media: the book. At the time of writing, *Upgrade Your Life: The Lifehacker Guide to Working Smarter, Faster, Better* was in its second edition.[1]

IPKAT
(http://ipkitten.blogspot.com/)

The IPKat is one of the best-known and most successful of all law blogs. As its name suggests, IPKat is about intellectual property (IP) law and is written mainly from a UK and EU law perspective. A mixture of written-word and pictures, it is read by IP owners, administrators, law students, practising lawyers, patent attorneys, trade mark attorneys and even judges. It sometimes receives information on IP law developments from the people involved in those developments, so is often the breaker of news. IPKat has a large international readership; as of May 2007 it was receiving over 25,000 visits per month and had over 1000 subscribers to its email list, together with an unquantifiable number of readers via RSS feeds (we discuss RSS later in this chapter).

IPKat was founded in 2003 – a time when most people had not even heard of blogs – by Jeremy Phillips and Ilanah Simon while both were members of the Queen Mary Intellectual Property Research Institute in the UK (Jeremy is now Research Director, Intellectual Property Institute and Ilanah has since been appointed to teaching positions at UK universities Brunel and UCL). They still write a lot of content for the blog but have since been joined by another academic, Johanna Gibson and a patent attorney, David Pearce.

Jeremy and Ilanah founded IPKat in part because of their frustration, as law teachers, at having to tell students to refer to legal texts when even the most recently published of those texts were often out of date. The blog was a way of allowing students to keep up to date with the latest developments; it

---

1   Gina Trapini (2008) *Upgrade Your Life: The Lifehacker Guide to Working Smarter, Faster* (2nd edition), John Wiley & Sons.

could report on a Court ruling even before it had made it into the law reports generated by the legal press.

Whilst the blog was not created for any purpose other than easily to distribute IP news, the writers tell us that it has significantly raised the profiles of the IPKat bloggers and is a springboard for the generation of revenue from activities as divergent as the holding of seminars on literacy for IP writers, the licensing of content, and collaboration in the production and promotion of commercial IP conferences.

COMMODITY TRADER
(http://commoditytrader.com/)

As you might have guessed from the name, this is a blog about commodity trading. The blog is regularly updated and contains concise and well-explained news on the commodities markets and the general financial markets. The blog's tag cloud indicates that Commodity Trader's pet subjects are futures and gold. The blog was named as one of the top 50 business blogs by UK newspaper *The Times* in 2007: http://business.timesonline.co.uk/tol/business/industry_sectors/media/article1923706.ece

These are just a few examples of business and professional blogs from the thousands in existence.

Blogs as an Information Resource

Blogs offer a new and easy way for businesses to stay in the know.

Until recently, businesses have relied on certain types of resource to keep up to date with industry developments:

- Subscription-only information services such as LexisNexis, which can take the form of periodically updated volumes of information in hard-copy form (e.g. law reports), and, more recently, searchable online websites and email updates;

- Newspapers;

- Industry journals and periodicals.

By and large, such information comes from a relatively small number of sources.

Blogs are an incredibly useful addition to these resources. In some fields, blogs arguably call into question the need for the traditional resources. Why buy a monthly trade journal when the trade blogs have already reported on the big issues and weeks ago?

Reading Blogs

What follows is an overview of the ways in which blogs can be used to find information and news about your chosen field.

ACCESS BY WEBSITE BROWSER

In their design, blogs are simply website pages, meaning that they can be viewed using a browser just like any other website. Microsoft Internet Explorer and Mozilla Firefox are two popular website browsers (most current operating systems come with a website browser as part of the package).

RSS NEWSFEEDS

Browsing any number of blogs or other sites trying to stay up to date with developments in your field soon becomes laborious. For this reason, most blogs feature *RSS newsfeeds*.

RSS stands for 'really simple syndication'. Dave Winer has come up with a succinct definition of RSS newsfeeds, describing them as:

automated web surfing ... It gets you more news for the time you put into using the Internet. If you don't want more news, then RSS is probably not for you. But if there are subjects that you are intensely interested in, and if the people covering the topics also offer the information in RSS, then your computer (or a Web site) can make web surfing a richer and perhaps more productive experience.[2]

Another good description of RSS comes from legal technology expert Dennis Kennedy, who says:

---

2   Dave Winer (2006), 'Let's ask what RSS is', *Scripting News*, 25 July, http://www.scripting. com/2006/07/25.html#letsAskWhatRssIs.

> With RSS and a news aggregator, each of the new posts from the blogs I care about automatically appears on my computer in an organized, easy to read-and-manage way in a news aggregator or news reader. I don't have to go to each blog individually. The new material from the bloggers I want to read, after I 'subscribe' to the RSS feed is available to me in one place at my fingertips. That's magical.[3]

Technology consultants Commoncraft have produced a great online video explaining RSS, which can be found at:

http://www.commoncraft.com/rss_plain_english

An individual RSS newsfeed usually consists of the headline of a blog item, plus maybe one or two sentences of text either summarizing the blog item, or quoting the first two lines of the item's text.

RSS newsfeeds can be viewed on *aggregator* software/services. With an aggregator, surfing through multiple blogs is replaced with viewing them all in one place. Aggregators allow you to choose the blogs that you are interested in and, once chosen, collect all the newsfeeds from those blogs together and display them in one place. An aggregator can display newsfeeds in a number of different ways, usually by showing the last few newsfeeds from each of your chosen blogs. Some aggregators will notify you when a new newsfeed appears, and show you which items you have not read. Some include search functions, so that you can search all the newsfeeds (and sometimes, the connected blog posts) in one go.

Podcasts (discussed in Part 2) use newsfeed technology, which means that many aggregators can also act as a handy way of keeping an eye on your favourite podcasts.

There are a lot of RSS newsfeed aggregators freely available. Here are some examples:

- **Greatnews** (http://www.curiostudio.com): A powerful and effective piece of software, available for download free of charge.

---

3   Tom Mighell and Dennis Kennedy (2006) 'RSS Resources You Can Use: Automated Web Surfing for Lawyers', *Law Practice Today*, November, http://www.abanet.org/lpm/lpt/articles/slc11061.shtml.

- **Google reader** (http://reader.google.com): A newsreader that is web-based rather than being software. Also free.

- **My Yahoo** (http://uk.my.yahoo.com): Another web-based newsreader. Again, free of charge.

The latest versions of the Firefox and Internet Explorer web browsers also include aggregators. At the time of writing, both are very basic, containing far fewer features than the specialist aggregators listed above.

Finding Blogs

FINDING BLOGS USING GENERAL SEARCH ENGINES

Because blogs are websites, you can find them using search engines such as Google (http://www.google.co.uk) and Ask.com (http://www.ask.com). A search along the lines of '[subject matter] blog' will result in a list of relevant blogs.

Although sometimes effective, this method is not exactly systematic or efficient. You are having to do the hard work and trawl through the search results, a lot of which will be irrelevant.

FINDING BLOGS USING BLOG SEARCH ENGINES AND DIRECTORIES

There are a number of search engines designed especially for finding blogs, of which Technorati (http://www.technorati.com) is probably the best known. Technorati's purpose is to record details of blogs and their content. At the time of writing, Technorati claimed to be tracking over 84 million blogs.

Another good general blog directory is Blogcatalog (http://www. blogcatalog.com/). Google also has a blog search facility (http://www.google. co.uk/blogsearch?hl=en).

Like the English-language parts of the wider internet, the English-language blogs are predominantly American. For readers based elsewhere, a good place to start is a blog search engine or directory specifically aimed at their particular location. Examples are:

- **The Australian Index** (http://theaustralianindex.com/);

- **Britblog** (http://www.britblog.com);

- **Kookkoo** (http://www.kookkoo.com/country/index.html) – a blog directory with listings by country.

There are also various blog directories on specific subject matters, and even blogs-on-blogs in particular areas. Here are some examples:

- **iBlogBusiness** (http://www.iblogbusiness.com/) – directory of business blogs;

- **Blawgreview** (http://blawgreview.blogspot.com/) – a regular report on what law blogs (known as 'blawgs') have been discussing;

- **Medworm** (http://www.medworm.com/rss/blogs.php) - a medical blogs filter and directory;

- **Music Blog Wiki's directory** (http://musicblog.wikia.com/wiki/Music_Blog_Directory) – a directory of music blogs.

ONE BLOG LEADS TO ANOTHER ...

Once you find a blog that you like, you will soon find others. This is because of a form of 'word of mouth' referral particular to blogs. With blogs, 'word of mouth' is translated into the common practice of bloggers providing links to other blogs. They do this:

- **Within their content**: For example, a report on the latest development will typically include references to reports on the same story by other blogs.

- **In 'blog rolls'**: These are lists of the blogs that the blog writers are fans of. If you like the blog you're reading, the chances are that you will find at least some of the blogs on the blog roll useful.

What are the Benefits of Blogging for Business?

Writing a blog can have various benefits for businesses. Here are some of the main benefits:

- Be your own publisher: in order to communicate your message to the world, you no longer need to understand HTML code to get it on a website, or go through your marketing people or PR agency.

- You have a ready audience of people waiting to read your blog: the internet is no longer something accessed by a minority of businesses.

Many are now familiar with it, and look to it for information. As we will see, the content of blogs is trawled by the search engines, meaning that your content will come up when someone searches on your subject matter.

- Speak with your own voice: by using a blog to distribute information, you are communicating directly with the outside world. In contrast with publicity done through marketing or PR agencies, blogging does not dehumanize your message. It's the genuine you, and that will be apparent to readers.

- Blogging is inexpensive: there are many ready-made platforms out there that you can use to blog. No expensive development costs need to be incurred, and no marketing agency needs to be paid to get your message out there.

- Blogging raises your profile: whilst many read blogs, there are still far more readers than there are writers. By blogging, your profile will inevitably be raised, both in the eyes of your industry peers and potential clients. Blogging gives you the ability to demonstrate knowledge on your subject matter in a direct manner.

- You can interact with clients and industry peers from your desk: from our experience, blogging is a brilliant and subtle form of networking, and can lead to strong bonds being formed between people in businesses who would not normally meet, and from around the world.

- Benefits from collaboration: with blogging, you can tap into a knowledge pool which is truly global. By writing a blog, you can contribute to this pool. In other words, you are collaborating with your business rivals in a way that benefits all without damaging any.

- You keep in touch with the technology used by those around you; simply by blogging, you will learn about many of the technologies that drive the internet, and will be aware of developments. This will help your business adapt and change with the times.

- Moving with the times: if you do not at least consider blogging (and the other types social media that we discuss in Part 2), you are soon going to look out of step with your staff and your clients. A number of drivers are already turning blogging into normal business practice: established publishers are producing blogs; marketing people are using blogs; established content management systems are incorporating blogging features; new graduate recruits within your business and those of your clients will almost certainly be existing users of blogs and social media. To put it another way, most young graduates have not experienced a time without text messaging and online interaction. In five years' time, blogging will be as normal for businesses as having a website is today. The culture will have changed: blogging will on balance be less geeky, less chummy, more commercialized. This mirrors what happened to the web itself only ten years ago.

- Blogs are a great tool for communication within organizations: see our chapters on collaboration and the use of blogs and social media internally in Parts 2 and 3.

Blogs Aren't Just Websites

Whilst blogs are websites, not all websites are blogs. Blogs contrast with 'standard' websites in a number of ways:

- Compared with blogs, websites tend to be more 'static', and updated only rarely. This is perhaps because whilst blog platforms are designed so that users can easily add new content, most websites are custom built and less easily editable. With most business websites, adding new information is often left to external web designers or the IT department. With a blog on the other hand, new information is entered into a simple form (usually with the title, the category, and the body of the article) and then put online. This may sound dry, but the effects for the user of such a system are quite dramatic compared with that of a traditional website.

- Blogs usually contain facilities allowing for easy filtering of content, for example by date, category, author or other attributes. Websites do not generally allow for content filtering unless specifically designed to do so.

- The content on blogs is normally from specific writers, even for business blogs. In contrast, business website content is not generally attributed to anyone in particular.

- On a blog, *individual pieces of content* are often linked to individual pieces of content elsewhere. With a website, links tend to be to particular pages on which the relevant content can be found.

- Blogs are interactive, in that they allow for readers to comment on content. On a well-received (or badly received!) piece of content, the feedback and further points made by readers can be just as important as the original content itself. Websites do not allow for this kind of writer–reader interaction.

- People can easily stay informed of the latest blog content by using technology such as RSS newsfeeds. We looked at RSS newsfeeds earlier in the chapter. From our experience, they are incredibly useful. Not many websites use such technology, so to find out what's going on from several websites, you have to invest the time and labour involved in clicking through each site.

Blogs versus Letters/Email

Most businesses use paper and email to communicate, both with clients and internally. Is keeping a blog 'better' than writing a letter or sending an email? As you'd expect, there isn't a yes/no answer to this question. It all depends upon what you want to communicate, who to and in what circumstances.

One highly relevant question that you might ask is: how many people do you want to communicate your message to? Where businesses need to communicate with numbers of people, blogging can often do a much more efficient job than a mass-mailshot or email.

For example, on a large project involving many people, huge amounts of emails/letters/memorandums are exchanged by the project team to keep each other up to date. This is a very inefficient and resource-intensive way of operating. Team members can be missed off the distribution list for a particular email/letter/memorandum. The content itself may be out of date before it's even been received by the rest of the project team. Managing all the various messages flying about can be a huge burden, both for the recipients (who have to file them all) and for the IT systems that have to process, forward, store and back-up the emails.

In this scenario, a blog can provide an attractive alternative to emails, letters and memoranda for team communication. All team members have access to the blog (which can be made private and secure), and so can read updates posted by colleagues and post their own. The blog can also be a forum for discussion, with team members able to comment on the information uploaded. Using a blog, the 'admin' burden can be immediately reduced, and real *communication* improved.

In contrast, where you are only going to communicate with a few people on a short-term basis (for example, a project), it's probably best to stick to tapping out an email or letter rather than using a blog.

There are also situations where another type of social media may be more suitable than a blog, or may be used in conjunction with a blog. We consider these other types of social media, and how they can be used, in Part 2. First, though, we need to look at how to create and write a blog.

Creating a Blog

If you wish to go down the blogging route, you must first:

- decide which platform to use; and

- set up your blog.

There are many blogging platforms available that allow you to set up a blog quickly, but there are a number of factors you need to consider when choosing a platform.

- **Budget**: Do you want to do this for free, or are you happy to spend some money on your blog? There are some good free blogging platforms out there, and lots of businesses use them, but they do have their disadvantages. With a free platform, the domain name will be, or will contain, the name of the platform itself, meaning that your brand does not get promoted as well as it would do using a (fee-charging) platform that allows you to choose your blog's domain name. In addition, you are likely to have less flexibility about the blog's design, limited or even no support from the platform provider and no scope to complain if the platform goes slow or breaks down. If you are happy to spend money, what is your budget? (Of course, the cost of running a blog can be met by income from the blog, but the set-up costs still need to be met up front).

- **Hosting**: Do you want the platform provider to host the blog, or do you want to host it on your own server? Hosting a blog yourself can be quite a burden; it involves renting server space, dealing with issues such as blog security (or paying your host to deal with this), and having to sort out technical stuff when you set the blog up. Hosting your own blog can, however, deliver a number of benefits, for example you get a full say in the resources available to the blog. If you want the blog to be able to deal with a huge number of concurrent users, or guarantee that it is incredibly fast loading, you probably have no choice but to host it yourself, or arrange the hosting yourself. Most of the fee-paying blogging platforms give you choice over whether you or they host, but with the free platforms it depends on the platform provider.

- **Reputation**: Do some research to find out what others think about the platforms you are interested in. If one platform has a reputation for instability – for example, it might recently have crashed for an entire day (they do sometimes) – go for one known for its resilience. If you don't do your research beforehand, you may only find this out when it's too late.

- **Getting technical (or not)**: To set up a blog using some platforms, you have to spend some time messing about with computer code, for example to design the page layout. If you are not able, or cannot be bothered, to program in the particular platform's language, go somewhere else. This issue tends only to apply to the open-source, free platforms.

- **Ease of use**: How easy is the blogging platform to use? This is something you will have to probably get a feel for when researching the platform's reputation.

- **Functionality**: Not all blogging platforms give you the same features. You need to think about what you want your blog to do, and whether the particular platform can deliver it.

- **Support**: If something goes wrong, or you need guidance, do you want to be able to contact a support team, or are you happy trying to find the solution yourself? If you want dedicated support, you will generally have to pay for it, either as a separate fee or as part of the periodic fee for use of the platform.

- **Internal use**: If you want the blog to be hosted internally within your organization, for use within your organization only, this will eliminate your ability to use platforms that insist on hosting your blog for you on publicly available websites.

- **The fun stuff – design**: As touched upon when discussing the budget factor, some platforms may give you little or no say in the design of your blog, and the level of control you have will vary a lot between platforms. Even if a platform offers you full control, before you decide to go ahead it is worth spending some time looking at other blogs based on that platform. Blogs produced on a particular platform tend to have a certain common 'look and feel', simply because few bloggers have the time or inclination to spend all day designing their blog. If a blogging platform comes with a selection of nice-looking standard designs, you might not think it worthwhile trying to invent one of your own.

- **Content portability**: At some point in the future you may wish to move blogging platforms. Can you easily move the content to another blogging platform? If not, you are potentially stuck with your current platform.

- **Accessibility/avoiding disability discrimination**: Websites being accessible to all is a big issue in the online world. More importantly, it is an ethical issue. A number of online standards have emerged for how content is displayed on the internet. For websites, the most established standard is WAI, the Website Accessibility Initiative (http://www.w3.org/WAI/). Although the official name for the accessibility standard WAI has produced is the Web Content Accessibility Guidelines version 1 (WCAG), these are usually referred to simply as WAI. Under WAI, there are three 'levels' of accessibility – A, AA and AAA – AAA being the highest level. Check if your desired blogging platform implements WAI, level AA or above.

Blogging Platforms

There are many blogging platforms to choose from. Before we look at the most popular, a disclaimer: blogging platforms are evolving all the time, so the information in this section should be taken as a rough guide only. By all means consider these platforms – we listed them because we either use them or know bloggers that do – but also do your own research too, and see if anything better has come along since we wrote this book.

FREE PLATFORMS

Blogger
(http://www.blogger.com/start)

Owned by Google, Blogger is probably one of the most well known and used blogging platforms. As well as being used for personal blogs, many group blogs host their blogs on Blogger.

Whilst we say below that Blogger has limited functionality, recently Blogger has started to gain features we would normally only expect to see in fee-paying blogging platforms. For example, you can now 'future date' your posts – specifying the date/time at which your post appears, therefore allowing you to plan the publishing of your posts in advance.

Advantages

Blogger has a quick sign-up process and set-up.

- It's simple to use.

- It works with various other party blogging services and software. For example, it links with Audio Blogger, a podcast service.

- It offers flexibility, with customizing templates and functions.

- If you have an internet-enabled mobile phone, Blogger Mobile allows you to submit blogs from your phone.

Disadvantages

- Functionality is relatively limited. However, various third-party services are available to plug in to Blogger to bring such functionality.

- Quality of templates is not great – at least, not for the business user.

- It does not allow you to put posts into categories, something that may rapidly annoy the business blogger.

- Blogs created on Blogger seem to load slowly, which may not create a good impression with readers.

- Blogs have a Blogger domain name, rather than their own individual domain name. This may be a factor if promotion of your brand is important.

Vox
(http://www.vox.com)

Vox is a personal blogging service created by Six Apart. Vox includes many of the features found in the social and professional networking sites that we discuss in Part 2. For example, a blogger can make 'friends' with another network, and join 'neighbourhoods' of bloggers. Privacy is an issue taken very seriously, with bloggers able to restrict who can view their blogs.

Advantages

Vox has a quick sign-up process and set-up.

- It's simple to use.

- It interacts well with certain third-party services. For example, it can import pictures from a Flickr account and display videos from YouTube.

- It offers a selection of design templates.

- Blogs created on Vox seem to load quickly.

- It has excellent privacy features.

Disadvantages

- Vox is a personal service, as we have said, few businesses seem to use it.

- There is limited ability to customize your blog design.

- Blogs have a Vox domain name, rather than their own individual domain name.

Drupal
(http://www.drupal.org)

At the other end of the scale to Blogger and Vox, Drupal is an open-source content management system. If you know what you're doing, you can use Drupal to create powerful and impressive blogs and websites. Unlike Blogger, you will need to host the blog yourself, so you need to find server space and sort out your own domain name.

Advantages

- Drupal is a powerful piece of software giving you all the versatility you could need.

- It's ideal for the technically knowledgeable user.

- It's an open-source system, meaning that you can edit the source code if you encounter problems or want more features.

- A community of other Drupal users are there to guide you through any issues you have.

Disadvantages

- Let's face it, Drupal is not an option unless you're technically skilled.

Wordpress
(http://wordpress.org/)

Wordpress is a highly popular blogging platform – according to Wordpress, the blogging software was downloaded almost 4 million times in 2007. Like Drupal, Wordpress is open source. Unlike Drupal, Wordpress is specifically a blogging platform, which is likely to reduce the level of technical complexity you have to get up to speed with. You will need to host the blog yourself.

Advantages

- Wordpress is free to use for both personal and commercial sites. Donations are encouraged.

- It's ideal for the technically skilled user.

- It's an open-source system and with a large community of developers.

- Loads of third party plug-ins and applications have been developed to work with and complement Wordpress.

Disadvantages

- The software could be better documented.

- Some have criticized Wordpress for being susceptible to comment spamming.

FEE-PAYING PLATFORMS

Movable Type

Operated by Six Apart, the people behind Vox, mentioned earlier, Movable Type is a popular open-source blogging platform, aimed fairly and squarely at the technically minded corporate user.

Advantages

- Movable Type is an advanced platform and possibly more suitable for the 'corporate user'.

- It has the widest variety of features.

- It's an open-source system.

Disadvantages

- It's another platform for the technically skilled. You need to be very 'computer literate'.

Typepad
(http://www.typepad.com/)

Also owned by Six Apart, Typepad is not open source. Typepad is aimed at both those with the skills and resources to host a blog themselves and those who don't want the hassle. Typepad is alleged to have a lot of customers in the media industry, but don't let that put other business bloggers off; this is a seriously powerful and easy to use platform.

Advantages

- Typepad has excellent templates, which can be further adjusted without any knowledge of HTML.

- It's easy to analyze how many people have visited your site.

- The cost is reasonable (between $50 and $150 a year), with a free 30-day trial.

- The software lets you see who has been linking to your blog, which also helps you keep up to date about what is being said online.

- There is a great support desk and online knowledge base.

Disadvantages

- Some teething problems and periods of downtime, though these seem to have been overcome more recently.

Setting Up Your Blog

You can set up a blog in under a minute. However, rather than just going ahead and creating a blog, it is worth first spending some time thinking about how you want your blog to look, and how users can interact with it. In this section, we discuss some of the key issues you need to consider when setting up a blog.

DESIGN

Blogging is all about self-expression, and the design of your blog is an important part of expressing what your blog is about.

You do not need to commission a website designer to lay out your blog. Many platforms provide a selection of template designs for you to choose from. Some allow you to customize these designs, or even create an entirely new design. If your platform allows it, it is worth taking the time to make your blog look different from the standard templates used by many other blogs.

Rather than doing the design work themselves, some business bloggers have paid website designers to do the job. The advantage of this approach is, of course, that you should (theoretically) end up with a blog that looks good and therefore helps preserve or increase your business reputation. If you go down this approach, check whether you will own the IP rights in the new design.

WHAT POLICY SHOULD YOU TAKE ON COMMENTS?

Blogs have the potential to allow readers to interact with the bloggers by making comments on blog posts. Most blogging platforms offer this facility; the question is whether or not you allow comments, and if you do, how you deal with them.

It is not surprising that one of the biggest concerns bloggers have centres on negative or inappropriate comments on their blogs.

These issues were considered in a blog post by Matt O'Neill who asked Michael Dillon, General Counsel of Sun Microsystems on his blog:

I have been advised by others to disable the comments field. The advice was based not on the possibility of libel, but rather that someone would say something negative about Sun, me or ... lawyers :)[1] My personal view is that part of the reason you blog is to create a wider network – to make connections (witness our email exchange). While it might be safer to disable the comment field, I think it would reduce the value of the blog.[2]

This is an important point – if you disable the comments field, your blog no longer has an element of participation. Furthermore, if you do allow comments, you should not delete a comment simply because it is negative. This could lead to a perception that you are censoring your readership. It is probably best to view negative comments as being an opportunity rather than a problem – they give the blogger the chance to prove their expertise, by publicly responding to the negative comment and challenging it.

It is a personal choice, but the writer's view is that comments should be allowed, because it shows that you are open to other views, and willing to allow exchanges on the blog. Some blogs are a great read because of the community of readers that discuss posts on them.

Part of good brand management is not allowing people to say gratuitously bad things about you on your blog. If you are going to manage your brand and allow comments, you need to moderate those comments. This involves reviewing comments when received by your blogging platform, and being able to choose whether to approve them for publication. Moderation lets you block inappropriate comments from appearing, but it does demand discipline: you should commit to reviewing and approving comments received at least once per day to avoid delays before comments appear on the blog.

Another consideration is whether your platform includes 'comment spam' prevention. Anyone with an email address now has to contend with junk email or 'spam' on a daily basis, and comment spam is the blog equivalent. This type of spam comes in the form of what purport to be comments on blog postings. To tackle this, many platforms use tests designed to eliminate 'spam bots' at

---

1   This is a smiley face in text form. The smiley and other text expressions such as :-(are sometimes called 'emoticons'.
2   Matt O'Neill (2006) 'Corporate Blogging: Legal opinion on External Comments', Modern Communicator, 14 September, http://activate.typepad.com/my_weblog/2006/09/corporate_blogg.html.

the time the 'comment' is submitted. One common type of test is to require the comment-maker to duplicate the letters or numbers within a graphical image. Given the current levels of comment spam, if your platform offers these features, it makes sense to use them.

A final point is that, if you receive a comment, you should commit to responding to it (by making another comment on the same blog post) within a reasonable period of time. By responding to comments, you can demonstrate that your blog is participatory, and help build up a community of readers who contribute to it. As previously mentioned, making comments yourself also provides an opportunity to prove your expertise in the relevant subject area.

IN IT FOR THE MONEY: GETTING REVENUE FROM YOUR BLOG

Except for a privileged few, blogging will not provide a massive source of income. There are, however, a number of ways that bloggers can make (some) money from their blogs.

Some blogs contain advertising that generate income for the blogger. Typically, the blog hosting the adverts will receive a small fee each time someone clicks on an advert. Alternatively, the fee could be based upon on the overall number of times pages featuring the advert are viewed. Having spoken to various bloggers, it is clear that these adverts are not the path to riches; even for a relatively popular blog, the income they generate will do no more than cover the cost of hosting the blog, or the fees charged by the blogging platform. Of course, if your aim is only to cover your costs, this may be all that you need.

The main advertiser on blogs is Google's Adsense service (https://www.google.com/adsense). At the time of writing, you could get up to three Google advert spaces on your blog. In these spaces, Google will place adverts based upon the content of your blog. For example, if your blog is about fishing, Google Adsense will display adverts for fishing goods and services. You can choose whether adverts are text based, image based, or both. You can gain further revenue by including a Google search within your blog and allowing Google to display sponsored adverts alongside the search results. Google keeps secret how much money from it receives from each advert and the amount that Google pays you is not open to negotiation.

If you are based in the USA, another advertiser that you can use is Blogads (http://www.blogads.com/).

As an alternative to generic Google adverts, you can choose to become an affiliate advertiser. This means hosting adverts for specific companies on your blog. How you earn money depends upon the affiliate scheme, but, is usually either in the form of payment when someone clicks on an advert on your site, or payment when someone actually buys something after clicking on an advert on your site. Amazon Associates is a large affiliate scheme to which many websites and blogs subscribe. It is run by online retailer Amazon (http://affiliate-program.amazon.co.uk/gp/associates/join/main.html). In the Amazon Associates scheme, payment is based upon sales made as a result of clicks on an Amazon advert on your blog, and is a percentage of the sales revenue. Another scheme is that of Linkshare (http://www.linkshare.com/uk/), which operates affiliate schemes for a number of big businesses, such as American Express.

Another way is to licence content to third parties. IPKat, the IP law blog mentioned in Chapter 1, generates income by doing this. Of course, you are unlikely to get income this way unless approached by an interested third party. This is not therefore an income stream to be counted on. This approach may also compromise your 'editorial freedom'; the third party will have its reputation to protect, and is therefore likely to want a say in what you can blog and/or how.

If you want to test the generosity of your readership, place a donation box on your blog. Through this, your readers can donate money to you. An example of a provider of donation boxes is Paypal (http://www.paypal.co.uk). Donation boxes are perfectly acceptable for personal blogs, but are unlikely to be a realistic option for most business bloggers, whose clients and prospective clients will not appreciate being begged off when the blogger should be earning its income from the business it is blogging about! However, business blogs could include a charity donation box, without embarrassment. Paypal provides charity donation boxes too.

In Chapter 5, we analyze blogging as a way of making money, and look at some of those that have succeeded in turning blogging into a business.

'I Still Don't Know Where To Start With Blogging!'

In this chapter we have done our best to summarize the main points about blogging, but we appreciate that learning from a book – especially on such a practical, non-intuitive topic – is often difficult. If you like the idea of blogging but do not feel confident enough to pay for a platform straightaway, the best thing to do is to minimize your risk by participating initially in a more limited capacity.

Rather than setting up a business blog right away, why not become a regular reader of existing blogs (ideally using an RSS newsreader)? This will allow you to familiarize yourself with how bloggers operate. Then take things a step further by creating a personal blog for yourself using one of the free blogging platforms that we discussed earlier. Set up the blog, write a few posts and keep it going for a month or two. If you do not want to blog in your own name, blog anonymously or under a pseudonym. You do not have to blog about your personal life; a blog can be on any subject, or indeed no particular subject at all.

This will quickly build your confidence as a blogger, and give you a good idea about whether in fact your business can or should blog.

Writing a Blog

Planning/the Psychological Battle

You can put new content on a blog at any time day or night. Unlike traditional media, there's no deadline for publication that you need to meet. This flexibility in timing can be a boon as well as a burden. 'If I can write my article at any time, I can put off doing it until this afternoon, or this evening' is one tempting thought. As with so many other tasks that can be pushed back, the evening becomes tomorrow, and then tomorrow becomes never. As with anything you want to achieve, the only answer is to just get on with it.

Many people who like the idea of blogging (but haven't got round to writing a blog) seem to spend more time thinking about how long writing a blog post will take than, our experience tells us, writing the actual blog would have done. We often get asked: 'How long does it take to write a blog?' The answer is: however long you've got. If you have got a packed day ahead and you have spotted a good story for your blog, whilst you may not have time to write a lengthy piece on the story, you will almost certainly have the few minutes it takes to put together a few sentences and a couple of links to other people's takes on the story. This is often as much as your (equally time-pressured) readers will need or want.

Of course, some stories or subjects justify a bit more investment of time. If you do not have the time to write the post all at once, make a start and come back to it later. A detailed piece will often only take half an hour. After all, you are writing pieces for a blog, not chapters of a book.

Coming back to your blog is probably the most important thing you can do as a blogger; if you do not write regularly, you will not enjoy blogging and you will not reach your target audience. Make writing for the blog a small but regular part of your working day, a pleasure and not a chore.

Once You've Started, Don't Stop

No blog looks worse, or sends a more negative message, than one that has fallen into disuse. If you are not disposed to writing a blog, do not start one. It looks unprofessional if you start a blog but do not take it forward.

Look Before You Leap

One good rule of thumb is to save a post without publishing and then revisit the draft at your leisure. If you are unsure about a draft post when you revisit it, rewrite or delete it. This is particularly useful for provocative or opinion pieces; getting these right could boost your reputation in your industry as a thinker, but the wrong tone or comment will do you no favours. Many professionals and businesses use this kind of technique in their everyday work of drafting letters and emails.

Peer-review before publishing a post may also come in handy if you are unsure your post is correct. If you do not have colleagues to discuss things with, you will find that other bloggers are often happy to look at your work. Of course, they may want to run things past you occasionally, but that's all part of the collaborative spirit of blogging and online discussion, and will lead you to positively build your industry and professional contacts.

Style and Substance

With blogs, what you say and how you say it is arguably much more important than the design and layout of the blog. Over time you will develop your own style of writing. Gina Trapini from Lifehacker told us: 'Write great content, and the audience and revenue will follow.' To get you started, here are some suggestions:

- **Keep your language simple**: Avoid technical or industry-specific jargon, and don't use long words just for the sake of it.

- **Conversational style?** Some blogs are written in a very conservational and chatty way, rather using than formal language. Some bloggers see this approach as being a good way of encouraging readers to react to content, getting a conversation between blogger and reader going. A conversational manner may help readers perceive that you really are writing the blog because you are interested in your subject matter, rather than the blog being some wizzy attempt to make you look cool and trendy by those clever folks in the marketing department.

- **Don't be overly commercial**: Blogs certainly have a place within the business spectrum and can be good way of marketing a business. However, a blog that takes an overly commercial approach is unlikely to make friends or influence people. If your blog's main focus is your products and services, your blog will simply be a glorified advert - not something that people will want to read.

- **Don't be too critical of others**: Generally try to be positive in tone. This isn't an excuse for blandness or fence-sitting, however. There is a lot to be said for being provocative (provided it's justified), and trying to generate interest in the work that you are doing. At the same time, remember that organizations have reputations that they need to protect.

- **Refer to other blogs**: We have already mentioned 'blog rolls' – lists of other useful blogs. Blog rolls are a good way of directing your audience to relevant resources. It is also good practice to refer to and link to other blogs within your content. If someone else has written a good article covering the same subject matter as you, include a link to their article. These practices mean that readers will see you as being at the centre of your industry or community, comfortable with your competitors. Readers will also come to use your blog as a resource for finding third-party information, which is also no bad thing. The bloggers you link to are likely to pick up on your comment and this might even lead to you striking up a dialogue.

- **Provocative posts**: Business and professional blogs such as law firm blogs tend to steer away from the provocative, but this does not mean that these blogs must be dull; a blog can be professional, but entertaining to read and hard-hitting.

- **Publish short posts regularly, not long posts occasionally**: Your readers are likely to have as limited time for reading blogs as you have for writing them, so put your time to best use. By writing short posts and publishing them regularly you will maintain a regular readership and may even been seen as being on-the-ball, the place to come to find the latest news and views about your subject matter. In contrast, long posts by their nature take longer to write, so you will publish less regularly and risk losing your readership unless your long posts are of consistently high quality. Another risk with long posts is that you simply will not want to write them, finding other more interesting things to do instead, and your blog ultimately becomes static and out of date.

Enhancing the Blogging Experience

Now that your blog is up and running, there are certain technologies and practices that can enhance your blog and maximize the benefits of blogging.

Drag in New Readers From the Search Engines: Search Engine Optimization

The very fact that you are writing regularly on your blog will ensure that you gain a regular readership over time. However, it's satisfying to gain new readers, and one way of doing this is by optimizing your blog content for the search engines. A few tweaks to how you write your blog posts can significantly increase the chances of people finding your blog during web searches. This is about making the most of knowledge about what people search for (when looking for information relevant to your blog's subject area) and how search engines collect information about blogs/websites.

Here are some key tips about how to optimize your blog content for the search engines.

TELL THE SEARCH ENGINES THAT YOUR BLOG EXISTS

The search engines compile their details of websites by 'crawling' across website pages. Therefore, at some point the search engines are likely to find your blog and start including it in search results. However, there is no guarantee of when this will happen.

Some search engines allow you to take control of the process by alerting them to the existence of your blog. For example, Google Webmaster Tools (https://www.google.com/webmasters/tools/siteoverview?hl=en_GB) allows you to register the details of your site with Google so that it begins 'crawling' it (if it isn't already), and to tell Google more about your site and its structure, so that it crawls it more efficiently and so that search results about your site are more accurate.

Improve the main titles of your blog

Someone who is searching for websites or blogs in your subject area, and who doesn't know about you already, will not be searching based upon your company name or your blog name; they do not have this information. The only way that they will find you on a search engine is if your blog comes up in the search results. You can improve the chances of this happening by improving the main titles of your blog. The main titles are:

- the tag line – this is the title that appears in the window of your web browser;

- the names of individual pages of your blog.

Change these to reflect the key words for your subject area. Avoid superlatives that do not describe what you do, such as 'brilliant' or 'professional'. Here are some examples:

- 'Criminal Law Blog – [blog name]' will do better than simply '[blog name] – high quality blog' or [blog name] – Criminal Law Blog'

- 'Forensic Accountants in London – [firm name]' will do better than '[firm name] – Forensic Accountants in London'

Note that by making these changes, you are not changing the brand of your blog; your blog name will stay the same. You are simply increasing the chances of people finding your blog in the first place!

Use key descriptive words prominently within your content

In other words, say what you're going to talk about before you talk about it. If your blog post is about a certain subject area, say that at the start of your post.

This is part of a wider subject known as search engine optimization (SEO). As the name suggests, SEO is about getting the maximum readers to a website simply through search engine results. The above tips barely touch upon the subject. Entire books, websites and marketing agencies are devoted to SEO. It's something that a lot of website owners can end up obsessed by – how to get in those extra readers? It should be noted that a lot of the suggestions we have given earlier in the book about blogging, such as writing regular quality posts to which others will want to link, are beneficial for search engine rankings and fit nicely within good SEO practice.

If the above hints have wet your appetite for more, and you want to make sure that Google knows your blog is top dog, we recommend:

- The Search Engine Optimization Journal blog (http://www.searchengineoptimizationjournal.com/)

- *Search Engine Optimisation for Dummies* by Peter Kent, part of the highly readable '*For Dummies*' series.[1]

It is worth noting that, to minimize the chances of people manipulating search results, the search engines regularly change the way that they rank websites as search results. There is therefore no fixed way of maximizing your blog's place in search engine results.

In conclusion, SEO is important for increasing readership, but not as important as the content of your blog; what is the benefit of having lots of people finding your blog on Google, only for them to discover that your blog doesn't have the content they are looking for? Do think about SEO, but don't become obsessed.

Advertise Your Blog Online

The way that search engines rank websites may change, but their willingness to take cold, hard cash in return for advertising your blog doesn't! Search engines rely on advertising as one of their main sources of revenue and you can pay for a sponsored advert on a search engine. These adverts are based on key words – the sort of key words we have just been talking about in the context of SEO. Here, your advert will be displayed on the search engine if someone searches for the key words you have registered. Most of these services, such as Google AdWords, charge on a 'pay per click' basis, meaning you only pay if someone clicks on your sponsored link.

Keyword adverts can be a good promotional tool, particularly in the early days of your blog.

---

1   Peter Kent (2006) *Search Engine Optimisation for Dummies* (2nd edition), John Wiley & Sons.

Use Pictures

Try to include graphics in your blog posts. Done well, this can make a blog look smart, add humour and generally make it stand out from the pack.

If you are going to use a picture, check that you are entitled to do so first. Many people seem to think that because an image is available on the internet, it is 'public domain' and they are free to use it. This is not the case; most images on the internet are protected by copyright, and someone will own the copyright to each image. Many photo distributors monitor the internet for unauthorized use of their images, so if you use an image without doing the due diligence you risk receiving an invoice or worse from the copyright holder.

By using a respectable online photo distributor you can avoid these sorts of copyright issues. A number of online sites contain images that you can use on your blog either completely free, or subject to a royalty fee or some other action such as notifying the copyright holder that you are going to use the image. Here are some places where you can get photos for your blog:

- **Stock.Xchng** (http://:www.sxc.hu): In our opinion this is one of the best online distributors. Stock.xchng contains over a quarter of a million photos, many of which can be used for free and some for a charge.

- **Able Stock** (http://www.ablestock.com): Gives you access to royalty-free photos for a subscription charge.

- **Shutterstock** (www.shutterstock.com): Another website supplying royalty-free photos for a subscription charge.

- **Creative Commons-licensed photo libraries**: Creative Commons is the name for a number of standard licences that people can use for their online images, audio and other media. These licences allow royalty-free use of media by others. Libraries of Creative Commons works therefore provide a good potential source of images for blogs. The official Creative Commons images library can be found at http://creativecommons.org/image/. Check the Creative Commons licence before you use an image – some licences prohibit 'commercial use', meaning that they arguably cannot be used on business blogs, even when those blogs are free.

Podcasting and Videocasting

Some people prefer to listen or watch than to read a piece of text, so why not give your blog some variety by adding podcasts and videocasts? We discuss podcasting and videocasting in Part 2.

Add RSS Newsfeeds

We have already seen that RSS newsfeeds are a great way of keeping up to date on the blogs you read without having to click through every single blog in your website browser. It comes as no surprise, then, that adding RSS newsfeeds to your blog will appeal to your readers.

Some blogging platforms come complete with RSS newsfeed functionality, but others do not. If your platform falls into the latter category, you will have to set-up your feeds using a third-party service.

Probably the most popular RSS newsfeed creator is Feedburner (http://www.feedburner.com). Owned by Google, Feedburner was used by over 500,000 websites as of August 2007. The service is free to use. When you add Feedburner to your blog, a Feedburner symbol is added to alert readers to its presence. Another popular choice is Feedblitz (http://www.feedblitz.com).

Make Your Blog Available By Email

Whilst the power and efficiency of RSS newsreaders makes them a popular option, there are many people out there who still like to receive their information updates by email.

Most blogging platforms do not have email services built in, but there are a number of good email services out there that will integrate with your blog. Feedburner, which we have just discussed in the context of creating RSS newsfeeds, is a popular choice and is free of charge. This is a great way of providing email updates without having to get involved in the process of creating the emails yourself. The service adds a 'Subscribe by email' button to your blog, and subscribers to the email list receive a daily summary of your blog's content. Subscribers can unsubscribe at any time. Feedburner Email gives the blogger access to the subscribers list, meaning that if you do not like the service or something better comes along, you can move to another email service with the minimum of pain. Again, if you do not fancy Feedburner then Feedblitz is a good alternative.

Widgets

Most blogging platforms allow you to incorporate small third-party utilities in to your blog design. These utilities are usually referred to as widgets (it saves all that stuffy 'third-party' talk).

There are a huge range of widgets available to bloggers. They range from the purely entertaining to the pretty useful. Here are some examples:

- **Search engine widgets**: Many blogs have Google widgets, which mean that your blog is searchable using the Google search engine. There is a variety of search widgets out there, including some specifically designed for searching blogs. A useful addition to any blog.

- **Social bookmarking widgets**: These mean that you can add information from your social bookmarking service (for example, del.ici.ious) to your blog. A real value-add to your blog if used well; if people are interested enough in what you say to read your blog, some will be interested to see what websites you have added as favourites recently.

- **Widgets that are purely promotional tools for third-party services**: For example, a widget for Amazon.co.uk. Like the entertainment widgets, these are more suited to personal blogs than business blogs.

- **Entertainment widgets**: An example is the Dilbert widget, which lots of blogs include. With this widget, the Dilbert cartoon-of-the-day is featured on your blog. Another example is the multitude of photo-of-the-day widgets, and widgets that display details of what music you've been listening to recently. These types of widgets should be used sparingly on a business blog.

- **Distribution widgets**: The RSS newsfeed and email tools we have just discussed, such as Feedburner and Feedblitz, can be added to many blogging platforms as widgets.

There are usually two ways to add a widget to your blog. The first way is by adding HTML code for the widget to your blog. The widget provider will supply this code on its website. This method can prove tricky, and if not done correctly, it can mess up the look of your blog (until you remove the widget code, which shouldn't prove difficult). The second way is to use your blogging platform's built-in widget-adding facilities. This can be as simple as selecting the widget from a menu and ticking to add it to your blog. Whilst the first way is pretty much always available unless your platform allows no customization whatsoever (highly unlikely), whether the second way is available and how easy it is depends entirely on your chosen platform.

Used well, widgets can liven up the user experience and make the blog more appealing and interactive. Used badly, widgets can quickly make a blog look confusing and cluttered!

See What Others Say About You

It is very easy to see what is being said about you online and who is referring to your blog. We have already discussed two methods of doing so in the context of looking for other people's blogs.

The most basic way of doing this is to use a search engine such as Google. Type in the name of your blog, your business or (for a bit of vanity) your name and see what comes up.

A more efficient alternative is to use a service designed specifically for the purpose. The most well-known of these services is Technorati (http://www.technorati.com). Technorati reports on who has been linking to your blog and gives blog rankings, which are calculated based upon the number of links to a particular blog from other blogs.

Some services do offer something more than this. One is the UK-based Market Sentinel, which claims to identify the crucial sources that companies and communicators should monitor in order to take business decisions (http://www.marketsentinel.com/). Those sources can be found amongst consumers, suppliers, competitors and government. The company offers its customers a range of benchmarking services so that they can compare their own authority and approval with that of their major competitors.

Comment On Other Blogs

Write the occasional comment on third-party blogs that you read. There are good reasons for doing this:

- By commenting on a blog, the blogger will be made aware that you read their content, will appreciate your contribution, and are more likely to refer their readers to your own blog.

- Readers of the third-party blog will also read your comment, which means that you will be seen as a commentator on that subject matter or industry. If you add comments to blogs read by your target audience, you will have made that audience aware of your name. For example, if your target audience is the creative industries, where better to make your name known than on arts and media blogs?

In addition to simply commenting on things that interest you, you can also write comments to draw attention to specific posts on your own blog. For example, if a popular blog has written about a subject from one angle and you've done so from another, go on to their blog post, comment that you've written on the same subject, and give a link to your blog.

Is Blogging Worthwhile for a Business?

CHAPTER 5

So far, we've outlined what a blog is and how to blog. To finish off, we ask the question that any prospective business blogger must consider: Is running a blog a worthwhile activity for a business? The small business blogger will have to justify the time spent blogging to themselves as a valuable activity; the 'wannabe' blogger within a large business will have to justify it to their colleagues and/or directors. The question is something that we've touched upon in various parts of the previous chapters, but here we devote all our attention to the subject. We consider the question from a number of angles.

Before we go any further, it is worth noting that the diverse world of social media does offer alternatives to blogs that some may find appealing. A good example is the hugely popular 'mini-blog' service Twitter, which we discuss in Chapter 8.

Blogging as an Information Distribution and Retrieval Tool

One of the things we have argued in the preceding chapters is that blogs represent an incredibly useful new information tool. Our view is that this is true both for the business running the blog and the blog's readership.

Whilst a blog will inform readers of news and other information from day to day, that information is effectively stored permanently on the internet. With the right links and menus built into the blog design, a blog can act as a permanent information resource. For example, Freeth Cartwright LLP uses the IMPACT® blog as a permanent store and distribution point for its guides to basic legal issues, for easy forwarding to clients who want information on a particular area. The firm feels that this alone justifies the existence of the blog, let alone anything else.

Of course, being located on the internet, not only can a blog be searched using the tools and facilities on the blog itself, it can also be searched using increasingly powerful independent search engines such as those on Google and Technorati, many of which provide facilities to allow you to embed their facility within your blog. For no price other than a little publicity for the search engine, your blog can offer its readership some very advanced search tools.

Blogging as a Form of Marketing

When it comes to marketing, what works comes down to what type of business you run. Who is your target audience? What do they respond to? How will they notice you? Of course, marketing is a subject in itself and not something that we can cover comprehensively here.

If a substantial proportion of your market regularly obtains its information from the internet, blogging is a potentially powerful form of marketing for your business. Equally, if a section of the media that is relevant to your market regularly looks to the internet for news on the industry, or to find industry figures to comment on events, blogging is an excellent form of marketing. Writing a blog may lead to industry journalists reading your blog and asking you for comments on developments or to write articles. If this occurs, your potential clients will start hearing about you in the industry press.

To look at it from another angle, if a substantial part of your market does not use the internet to obtain its information and to look for new suppliers (that is, you), blogging is not a great form of marketing.

The benefits of blogging set out above apply more to small businesses than large. With a large business, if the target market has already heard about them and the industry press is already writing about them, they obviously do not need a blog to achieve these goals. With these type of businesses, the question is: Can blogging achieve further marketing benefits? For example, could writing a blog or encouraging staff to write blogs lead to the market seeing these businesses in a different light? This tactic appears to have caught on at Microsoft, which encourages its resellers to write blogs about the Microsoft products that they sell and their dealings with Microsoft.

Blogging as a Profile-raising Tool

If your industry peers obtain their information from websites, writing a blog can be a good way of raising your profile in the industry; your peers are likely to find your blog (or be told about it by you!), and see what you have to say. Your peers may even become regular readers, particularly if your blog keeps them up to date on industry developments! Additionally, if your industry press starts asking you for comments on issues as a result of seeing your blog, your industry peers will see these quotes in the industry publications that they read. Both of these things will result in your profile being raised in the industry.

Whilst having an increased profile will not directly result in new clients, it could have less obvious but more long-term benefits, such as:

- You might be invited to tender for work by potential clients who might not have otherwise considered you – because they wouldn't have heard of you!

- For individual bloggers, being 'names' in the industry could make it easier to find jobs elsewhere. This is either a threat or a benefit, depending on your attitude towards your blogging staff.

- Becoming a media commentator – when journalists look for content for news stories, they often turn to the internet and blogs in particular to find the 'expert opinion'.

Gina Trapini from the Lifehacker blog told us:

As a direct result of the site, I've been invited to judge technology competitions, write a monthly magazine column, and cited as a source in mainstream media outlets like the *Wall Street Journal* and the BBC.

Like blogging as a marketing tool, whether blogging will be a useful profile-raising tool depends on whether your industry and/or industry press uses the internet to get their information.

Blogging as a Way of Networking

If you blog, it is inevitable other bloggers will notice you, both within your industry and in connected fields. Starting often with either comments on each others blogs or links to each others' blogs, people with common interests will start communicating who might not otherwise have known of each others' existence. For example, the various contributors to the blog from which this book originated first started communicating with each other because of their blogs.

Blogging is therefore a subtle form of networking. It can lead to people starting to communicate and work together who would never have met through traditional networking routes, such as lots of people in a big room, simply because being in one geographic location is not a requirement. Location and even time zone are no barrier to bloggers networking.

Blogging's networking potential should not be overstated, however. If you want to get new clients and referrals through networking, there is no substitute for going to 'real' networking events. In terms of online networking, we will see in the Part 2 that there are online services specifically dedicated to helping you keep in touch with existing contacts and make new ones. In conclusion, whilst blogging can indirectly lead to networking, and from there maybe some good opportunities, this is a nice side-effect rather than a major reason for becoming a blogger.

Blogging as a Revenue-generating Activity

We have already said that a select few can blog for a living. Here, we will give examples of those people and look at how they do it.

DARREN ROWSE

Darren Rowse earns a living writing the ProBlogger blog (http://www. problogger.net) and a number of other blogs. Darren began blogging in late 2000. In his post 'Becoming a ProBlogger' (http://www.problogger. net/archives/'006/01/'5/becoming-a-problogger/), Darren writes that he starting blogging as a hobby, initially blogging about whatever took his interest.

We've already discussed using adverts to bring in revenue, and said that for most people this is all that such adverts will do. Darren used Google advertising to cover his costs, and initially this is all that such advertising did. However, by May 2004, such was the popularity of his blogs that Darren was earning $1,000 a month from Google adverts. The amount of time that Darren spent blogging gradually rose to 2 days a week. By 2005, Darren was blogging full time as well as being employed in another job, and Darren continues to blog full time. At points during this journey, Darren was writing up to 50 posts per day. Not something to be taken on lightly!

Aside from the fact that you can make money from blogging, the most interesting thing about Darren Rowse's story is the major drop in income he reports at one stage. As we saw in the section on SEO in Chapter 4, Google regularly changes its search engine rankings criteria, and as a result of one change Darren's blogs 'virtually disappeared' from the rankings. This resulted in many less visitors to his blogs, and as a result Google paid him much less advertising revenue. The moral of this story? *Don't rely too much on advertising revenue.*

In terms of making money from blogging, Darren's commentary gives the message *blogging for an income takes time.* His blog says: 'while there are stories around of people making good money from blogs much faster than I have, from what I know of the many bloggers that read this blog my own increases have been faster than most'. In other words, there's no hard-and-fast rule for the amount of money you're going to get from blogging, and don't count on receiving any particular regular sum. Darren's 'Becoming a ProBlogger' piece and his various contemporary posts on 'ProBlogging' should be mandatory reading if you are interested in making a living from blogging.

JASON CALCANIS AND BRIAN ALVERY

Jason Calcanis and Brian Alvery followed much the same approach as Darren Rowse to make money from blogging: they set up numerous blogs. They did this under the umbrella of a company set up for the purpose, called Weblogs, Inc. (http://www.weblogsinc.com). Weblogs, Inc. was launched in 2003. Within three years, the company was operating over 50 blogs. At the time of writing, the company had over 50 active blogs, many of which are incredibly popular, such as the Engadget series of blogs (http://www.engadget.com). AOL, the US media and technology company, bought Weblogs, Inc. in 2005 for a reported $25 million. Like Darren Rowse, Weblogs. Inc. makes money from blogging through advertising revenue; the more times its blogs are viewed, the more money it is paid by the advertisers.

KEVIN O'KEEFE

Kevin O'Keefe is the founder of LexBlog. LexBlog is a consultancy and service provider to lawyers and other professionals who blog or want to blog. Kevin is a former US lawyer, who quit law to blog and run online businesses aimed at lawyers. Kevin uses his blog, Real Lawyers Have Blogs (http://kevin.lexblog.com) as a tool for marketing LexBlog. With Kevin, therefore, whilst blogging does not itself bring in the money, it is a crucial marketing tool for LexBlog.

We deliberately left the above examples until the end for two reasons:

1.   They are not a representative sample of bloggers. Considered on their own, they make blogging seem a must-do activity that is worth spending all your time on because it's bound to bring in loads of money, ticking all the boxes. As we've seen, this is not going to be the case for most businesses, who will be best off keeping a blog alongside their other activities.

2.   Despite the caution we've just expressed, the achievements of these bloggers demonstrate what can be achieved by blogging.

Conclusion

Blogging is for most businesses going to be a worthwhile activity, but what makes it worthwhile will vary from business to business. When asked about the benefits that writing the Lifehacker blog had brought her, Gina Trapini told us:

Too many to count! Most notably two book deals, magazine bylines, friends, some great co-workers, and a whole lot of knowledge and experience managing an online community and publishing outlet.

For most businesses, running a blog should not be considered the sole marketing activity that the business performs, and the time invested in blogging should reflect this. Whatever else a blog does, our experience and those of the other bloggers we have spoken to is that running a blog leads to a massive raising of profile and reputation, and the indirect opportunities that blogging brings makes the exercise worthwhile.

Social Media

Introduction to Social Media

Important as they are, blogs are just one many forms of social media. The chapters in Part 2 consider some of the others.

It goes without saying that the more familiar a business is with the various types of social media, the better placed it will be to make the most of them:

- as means of communicating with clients and potential clients;

- as tools to improve efficiency;

- by being able to react rapidly and appropriately if a client or supplier begins a social medium in its own business.

In Part 2, our aim is to make you aware of the various forms of social media and get you started on the road to using those that interest you or are relevant to your business.

What is 'Social Media'?

The term 'social media' is credited to Chris Shipley, co-founder of Guidewire Group, a San Francisco-based company that researches and reports on technology trends. The term is used to describe online tools and utilities that allow:

- communication of information online; and

- participation and collaboration.

The following technologies fall within the 'social media' category:

- blogs

- professional and social networking sites

- wikis

- podcasting and videocasting

- virtual worlds

- social bookmarking.

This is a non-exhaustive list.

We discuss each of the main forms of social media in the chapters that follow, illustrating their uses and discussing some of the leading platforms. Although we have categorized certain services as belonging to a particular social media form, many of these services contain aspects of other types of social media. The competition between service providers for new users is relentless, and this has lead to many services seeking to provide various social media services under one umbrella brand, and in some instances even combine them.

For example, many blogging services contain features from other social media such as the ability to send private messages to other users. A second example is Flickr, which we include in the 'consumer-content distribution' category (see Chapter 8). Flickr is not just a method of distributing content, it also contains social networking features and links easily with various blogging technologies.

So Many Choices ... So Little Time

Do a quick internet search for wiki services, podcasting services and any other type of social media services, and you will find a massive selection available. There are seemingly hundreds of platforms out there – too many for a book, let alone a few chapters. By the time this is published, many of the services will have evolved in expected directions, some will have merged together and others will have disappeared altogether. This is an inevitable weakness with any book on emerging technologies.

This part does not therefore attempt to list every single social media platform. Instead, for each of the main categories of social media we discuss the main services that existed at the time of writing. Whilst individual platforms will over time rise and fall in popularity, and change in character, the social media concepts that they implement will stay constant (although we are likely to see new concepts develop). Therefore, a discussion of the social media platforms current at the time of writing is worthwhile, even if just to give a feel for what the social media concepts are about.

Should you join and use each of the services that we discuss in Part 2? The answer has to be no; just as business people do not have the time to attend every single networking event in their local city, they will not have the time to use every type of social media that is relevant to their industry. We therefore suspect that most business people with an interest in maximizing the opportunities presented by social media will end up using:

- one professional networking service;

- one consumer-orientated media service; and

- depending on their target audience and/or information needs, one or two of the other types of social media such as a wiki, podcasting or videocasting service.

Just as with 'real-life' networking and marketing opportunities, the only ways to see whether a particular type of social media platform is good for your business are to:

- see what other people say about particular services;

- try them out for yourself.

In the chapters that follow, we seek to provide you with the former; only you can do the latter. Like most things in life, what you get out of anything you try will largely depend upon what you put in. It's not enough to simply sign up for a particular social media platform. Once signed-up, give it a trial for a week and actively experiment with its features. See what colleagues and maybe even clients think of what you produce using the platform.

To save time using your chosen social media service, you can use a social media aggregator. We look at these in Chapter 14.

Professional Networks for Businesses

There are a number of services designed to allow businesses to network online with other businesses, some of which serve specific industries. A few of these of these are described in this chapter.

LinkedIn

LinkedIn is probably the most popular business-to-business social networking site. If only for the sheer number of other business users, if you are going to use just one professional networking site, make it LinkedIn.

The service claims to have more than 13 million members from 150 industries. According to the blog of leading technology thinker Guy Kawasaki, all of the US Fortune 500 companies have employees using LinkedIn, and for the overwhelming majority this includes director-level people (http://blog. guykawasaki.com/2007/01/ten_ways_to_use.html). In May 2007, the service was awarded best social networking site and best services site in the Webbys web awards.

Based on our experience as users, the majority of LinkedIn members are based in the USA, although there is a sizeable membership from the rest of the world. Users are a mixture of senior-level people from large organizations and directors of small businesses.

LinkedIn has a number of potential key uses, which we set out below.

MAIN USES OF LINKEDIN

Maintaining your contact list ... or letting your contact list maintain itself

Even if used for nothing else, LinkedIn is a great way of maintaining your list of professional contacts, perhaps as a backup to the lists of contacts in an email system such as Outlook. The key advantage that LinkedIn has over other contact list systems is that the details of your contacts are kept up to date by the contacts themselves. So if someone moves from one business to another, you keep them as a contact and get their new phone number and email address when they update them on LinkedIn. Of course, LinkedIn can only list those contacts that are also LinkedIn members.

Establishing contact with potential clients through your existing contacts

LinkedIn shows you who your contacts have in their contact lists. If you want to approach a contacts' contact, LinkedIn allows you to do so by asking your own contact for an introduction. This means that you are not cold-calling a potential client; instead, you are being recommended to them by someone they already know.

Implied recommendation of your services

If a potential client knows through LinkedIn that you do work for one of their friends, suppliers or customers, that may assist in securing that client. It's an implied recommendation of your services.

Let your contacts tell world how great you are

Getting recommendations and references out of contacts is difficult at the best of times, but LinkedIn seeks to make this as easy as possible and to maximize the benefits of those recommendations.

Contacts can recommend you on LinkedIn, and the recommendations appear on your profile. You aren't exactly going to be harmed if a potential client or employer sees those recommendations.

Of course, it's nice to recommend your contacts to others too. Writing a recommendation can take as little as a few minutes, a small price to pay for the gratitude you will receive from your contact!

Publish your CV/resumé online

You can create a detailed LinkedIn profile, which is effectively on online CV/resumé. If you want to make your profile viewable outside the confines of LinkedIn, the service will create a public web page based on your profile. According to some search engine experts, LinkedIn profiles receive high search rankings on search engines such as Google. In other words, a potential client who searches for information about you online is likely to come across your LinkedIn profile pretty quickly.

To get the most out of LinkedIn you need to fully complete your profile and make sure it's available for viewing by all other members. Put in lots of detail. LinkedIn allows you to see who's been looking at your profile, which can make interesting reading.

Show the world how great you are – answer questions

Another feature that can be used to raise your profile is LinkedIn Answers. This allows members to ask a question, which will be published on the LinkedIn Answers page. There are multiple categories of questions.

Any LinkedIn members can submit an answer to a question. Answers are published for all LinkedIn members to see, and the asker of the question will be sent your answer and given your details. Your answers can also be found on your LinkedIn profile. This is a great way of demonstrating your expertise to other LinkedIn members.

If you answer a lot of questions in a short period, you may find that LinkedIn has listed you as a 'top expert' on the front page of Answers.

So that you do not have to keep returning to LinkedIn to check for questions, LinkedIn allows you to subscribe to Answers by RSS newsfeed (see Chapter 1 for more information about RSS newsfeeds).

Finding, advertising for jobs and head hunting

One of the main things that LinkedIn is used for is job hunting and head hunting. The site has a specific service for job searching and advertising.

Employers can post details of jobs on the service, and these are searchable by those looking for new jobs. Many major organizations use LinkedIn to advertise jobs, particularly in the IT sector. On the flip-side, recruiters can use the site to find people appropriate for a particular position.

Of course, if you are seeking a new job, it's a good idea to create a comprehensive profile (see above).

Research a person, an organization or an industry

You can look up which employees of an organization are on the site, who their contacts are, and by doing this learn more about that organization. If you want to find out more about trends or issues in a particular industry, LinkedIn members who are part of that industry may be willing to answer your questions. Similarly, if you are going to meet someone for the first time you can see if they are on LinkedIn and, if they are, find out more about them in advance.

Set up a group

LinkedIn provides a feature for groups called, not surprisingly, LinkedIn for Groups. To see how Groups worked, the writers set up a LinkedIn Group for a professional organization of which they are members..

Setting up a group allows for communication between group members, but the facility is not particularly interactive. It does not provide tools for downloading the membership list or sending messages to all members, or any ability to chat on-screen.

The process for creation of a LinkedIn group is tedious: you must email a request to LinkedIn and they will set the group up for you. This can take a month or two.

COST

A basic version of LinkedIn is available free of charge. This version limits your ability to approach people outside your existing contacts, but has all the functionality that most people will need. A subscription-based version allows you to do this, although it is mainly head hunters who pay for this privilege.

XING

Xing (http://www.xing.com) reportedly had 2.13 million users as of 31 March 2007. Its target audience is 'business people worldwide'. The service, operated by German company Open Business Club AG, reported revenues of €3.93

million during the first quarter of 2007. On its website, it says: 'No two people are more than six degrees apart. Put theory into practice and benefit from your XING network.'

Xing's potential uses are very similar to those for LinkedIn. The service is centred around networks of contacts, and allows you to see who your contacts have listed as contacts. Like LinkedIn, Xing offers either a free service or a subscription service, the free service providing the user with less functionality. Also like LinkedIn, Xing has a Marketplace service for advertising for and searching for jobs. Going further than the LinkedIn equivalent, Marketplace automatically suggests jobs to users. The service allows you to see what jobs are being advertised by your contacts, and allows you to recommend a job to one of your contacts. Finally, like LinkedIn, you can use all of these features to research industries or organizations.

As with LinkedIn, there are groups – here called forums – focused on particular subjects. Joining forums and interacting with members is a good way of meeting new contacts and potentially getting new business. Xing has over 25,000 forums.

Ryze

Ryze (http://www.ryze.com) is a relatively small professional networking site, with 250,000 members across the world. The service was founded by Adrian Scott, one of the investors in the music-on-demand service, Napster.

As with the professional networking sites discussed so far, Ryze offers a free service and a subscription service. Whilst Ryze offers services similar to both LinkedIn and Xing, it seems to be more oriented towards job searching/ advertising and, in its classified section, advertising for other goods and services. The membership of Ryze appears to be primarily American and, with such a small overall membership, this is probably not going to be the first port-of-call for those new to professional networking.

As with all these services, Ryze may well benefit from future growth in membership and functionality. It certainly does more than either LinkedIn or Xing to promote its services on its home page, which is full of quotes, endorsements and excerpts from press coverage.

Inventube

Inventube (http://www.inventube.com) is an industry-specific networking service aimed at inventors and people in connected industries such as patent agents and investors. On the Inventube website, the service is described as an 'online network to connect inventors with manufacturers, attorneys, agents, scouts, investors, and others who can help bring your ideas to market ... quickly!'

The service launched in 2007 and, at the time of writing, was at a relatively early stage of development, with not all features active. It contains the following features:

- a member search and contact facility

- an online directory of businesses

- access to patents posted on the site by their inventors

- discussion groups

- a blog hosting service for businesses

- the service is free of charge.

Consumer-oriented Media

Consumer-driven sites, often called 'Web 2.0', have become the rising stars of the internet in recent years, ranking among the most popular sites on the web. A lot of the innovations in social media have originated on the consumer-driven side.

By creating online communities that can be actively shaped by the user, consumer-driven media has given web users great freedom over what content they view, where they access it and from whom they receive it. Consumer-orientated media is also an important topic for both those businesses whose target audience uses such media, and because business people have started to use some consumer-orientated services to network and get new clients online. The sites described below are, at the time of writing, some of the more popular sites.

Social Networking Sites

As the terms suggests, social networking sites allow people to network online in a primarily non-business way. The most popular sites deliberately blur the boundaries between different types of social media in the battle for popularity, including blogging and content distribution features. Some are also beginning to blur the boundaries between social networking and professional networking. All are, at the time of writing, free of charge for users unless we state otherwise.

FACEBOOK
(http://www.Facebook.com)

A combination of powerful networking facilities and entertaining features has led to Facebook becoming one of the most popular, and talked about, social networking sites. By the time this book is published, Facebook's status as the 'site to be seen on' may be over, but at the time of writing, it remains one of the most popular social networking sites.

When Facebook started, it was aimed at teenagers and young adults at college and university. A few years ago, *USA Today* reported on a survey of American colleges that found that Facebook was the second most popular thing amongst college students, just as popular as drinking![1] Now, however, teenagers and young adults are just one part of the Facebook demographic. Since opening the doors to everyone, the popularity of Facebook has shot up dramatically. Facebook has a smart interface, a wealth of features and a huge number of users, all of which have made it increasingly popular with professionals.

With Facebook, the emphasis is on users' identities being authentic; fake identities are frowned upon and are deleted by the Facebook administrators. Facebook's use of real names gives it a professional and grown-up feel, which is part of its appeal for business users.

Your Facebook identity consists of your real name, the details of the school, college or university you are at or last attended, your job and your geographic area. To illustrate how this works, let's take this author's use of Facebook as an example. Because the author, a lawyer, is based in Nottingham, on Facebook he is in the Nottingham network, along with about 34,000 other Facebook members. As he has a graduate email address from his university, he can join his university's Facebook 'network', allowing him to interact with the members of that network. The way that Facebook is set up allows the author to easily find and network with former university and college friends, current and former colleagues, other lawyers, and even clients. The above example hopefully gives some idea of the wide range of social contacts that Facebook facilitates.

Before we put our serious face on and discuss how Facebook is relevant to professionals, it is worth looking at the entertaining side of Facebook, because it is this side that makes people use the service on a regular basis:

- There are a number of slightly frivolous features built into Facebook. One core feature is the status update. You can write a brief sentence or two on what you are doing now, and Facebook will broadcast this update to your Facebook friends. Of course, it also tells you the status updates of your friends. Because you can write whatever

---

1   Mike Snider (2006) 'iPods knock over beer mugs', *USA Today*, 7 June, http://www. usatoday.com/tech/news/2006-06-07-ipod-tops-beer_x.htm.

you want for your update, status updates are both a very useful and entertaining feature. Just as you might get some useful news like 'Jim is at a conference 'til tomorrow', you might also get 'Rachel is thinking, therefore she is'. The possibilities are almost endless. Another core feature is the ability to upload photos, and tag people in those photos, so that your friends can find the photos that they are in.

- Facebook allows third-party developers to create applications that run within Facebook, taking advantage of its networking features. This has led to the spawning of hundreds of applications, many of which are a complete gimmick: paint programs, Pacman, Zombie attacks – the list goes on. But there are also more and more third-party applications useful to professionals, and we will discuss these later.

Going back to the business side of things, Facebook has a number of features that make it useful to the professional. Two important features are groups and the ability to blog.

Groups

There are thousands of groups on Facebook, most of which have been created by users. Many are purely 'social' (for example, discussing music), but there is a range of groups that are useful to professionals. One example is the Business to Business Networking Club (B2B), which has 170 members, and is about being able to 'promote your business without having to attend a 7am breakfast meeting' (to quote the group description), an aim that the author finds very appealing! B2B aims to have no more than one person from any particular specialism unless there is a difference in geographic region. The group was created by Benji Stern, a London-based mortgage adviser. B2B is still new, but Benji has told us that he's already got some potential business from people in the group. B2B is a brilliant example of the potential of social networking for businesses.

Other examples of Facebook business groups are:

- the new and growing Advanced Contract Lawyers group, aimed at trainee and qualified contract lawyers from across the world;

- the various groups for employees of specific businesses, such as US outfit A1 Car Rental and Welsh company Acen;

- AC Ellis Photography, a group set up for interaction between company employees and clients. (This company appears to understand the potential of social media – it also has a very good blog!)

As well as Facebook groups that aim to generate business for their members, there are also groups designed to allow professionals to talk with their fellow professionals around the world.

Blogging

Facebook allows you to write notes. Your Facebook friends are alerted to these notes and can respond to them. This means that a note on a particular issue can result in a whole discussion over that issue. Whilst the Notes feature is pretty good, more useful to the serious blogger is the ability to import the content of an external blog. This means that there's no need to duplicate your blogging efforts, and your Facebook friends are alerted to your external blog.

Third-party applications

There are an increasing number of third-party applications being developed that have relevance to professionals. At the time of writing, Facebook had only been open to third-party developers for a few months. However, even at this early stage there were various blog aggregation, recruitment, messaging and organizational applications emerging.

Business opportunities with Facebook

So what opportunities for businesses does Facebook present? The first is the ability to network with fellow-professionals and potential clients. If you put in the time and effort, Facebook can be a very good place to network and maintain your professional relationships. Some professionals we have spoken to go as far as to say that Facebook is better for networking than LinkedIn (see Chapter 7). Whilst LinkedIn allows you to build up a list of contacts, Facebook takes things one step further by actively communicating with them.

There are a couple of issues with using Facebook for professional networking. The first is that the service is primarily designed for social networking. You chat with your friends and have a bit of fun. Do you really want to mix up your friends with your business contacts? Such mixing potentially means that your business contacts know far more about you than you'd really want. On the other hand, if you're relaxed about your friends and business contacts mingling, Facebook provides a fun and relaxed way of interacting with both.

The second issue is that, during 2006–07, a lot of organizations blocked access to Facebook because it is perceived as so addictive, and therefore a potential time waster. This is not something that we consider a big problem; your professional contacts are never going to all be using the same online services, and even with access blocked in some offices, a huge number of professionals continue to use Facebook.

The second opportunity is to raise your business's profile through advertising on Facebook. Facebook advertising is geared towards allowing businesses to either advertise to specific college or university networks, or to advertise generally. At the time of writing, only the more youth-oriented brands – the Redbulls of this world – appear to be taking advantage of the potential. However, it cannot be long before a professional firm sets up a Facebook campaign aimed at drawing the attention of business users or potential employees.

MYSPACE
(www.myspace.com)

MySpace allows registered users to (amongst other things):

- have a page on which they display information about themselves;

- interact with other MySpace users through chatting on each others pages;

- make other people on MySpace 'friends';

- join groups based on their interests;

- publish 'bulletins' of their latest news;

- keep a blog;

- customize their page layout;

- upload photos, videos and music.

Whilst the number of users varies wildly depending on what source you read (somewhere between 21 million and 75 million unique visitors) and with over 100 million registered users, at the time of writing it is largely undisputed that MySpace is the most popular of the social networking sites. Although widely perceived as being a website used by teenagers, a study in 2006 by comScore Media Matrix (http://www.comscore.com/press/release.asp?press=1019) found that just over 50 per cent of visitors to MySpace were aged 35 years and over. Our impression from joining the site and using it, however, are that most of the users are teenagers and young adults, contradicting this statistic. Chatting with your kids and their friends will readily confirm this.

Probably because of its popularity, the creator of MySpace, Intermix Media, was bought by News Corporation in 2005 for a reported $580 million. Since the purchase, News Corporation has developed the site to maximize its revenue-generating potential through placing advertising on the site. In 2006, Wall Street analysts controversially estimated that MySpace could be worth between $10 billion and $15 billion by 2009. Whether or not this estimate becomes a reality is , for our purposes, almost irrelevant; even if its value does not grow by anywhere near that much, MySpace still demonstrates the potential business benefit to be gained from social networking sites.

Whilst MySpace demonstrates business benefits for News Corporation, what other types of businesses can gain from it? The obvious answer is businesses providing products and services that the MySpace demographic will want to purchase. The two obvious business types that should be on MySpace are:

- **Musicians**: MySpace is now an established method for bands and musicians to communicate with their fans and to get more fans. A typical band's MySpace page will have a few songs available to play, some pictures of the band, a space for fans to place their comments and a 'latest news' bulletin about the band.

  MySpace Music, the directory of bands with pages on the site, lists (at the time of writing) over 8 000 bands. As a method of communication for bands, the site seems a success. For example, to pick an old band that the author happens to like, the Pixies' MySpace page has been viewed over 1.7 million times, and 28 000 comments have been made about it. One of the songs that the band has placed on the page, 'Where Is My Mind', has been played 1.4 million times. For new bands, having a MySpace presence is a crucial step on the road to getting a following and attention from the record companies. In 2006, an unsigned band called Koopa got into the UK top 40 without having a recording contract in place. As well as playing live, the band had done some online marketing, including having a MySpace page.

- **Businesses selling products/services aimed at young people**: Again, MySpace offers a way of directly communicating with the target audience for these sorts of businesses.

There are two ways that a business can raise its profile on MySpace: advertising and having a MySpace page.

Advertising

At the time of writing, the UK MySpace site contained the following types of adverts:

- throughout the site, video adverts for computer manufacturer Apple;

- adverts for satellite television provider Sky (owned by MySpace's parent company, News Corporation);

- adverts for movies, including a promotional competition;

- adverts for a mobile phone company;

- sponsored links, the particular links being dependent upon the particular part of MySpace you are using; for example, in the blog section, I received adverts for various blogging services.

These are clearly products and services that would appeal to MySpace users.

The cost of advertising on MySpace varies depending on the type of advert and where it is placed. According to one report in 2006 (http://blogs.zdnet.com/ micro-markets/index.php?p=89), it costs about $1 million per day to advertise on the MySpace front page, although because News Corporation keeps this information confidential – and again, reports vary wildly in terms of the figures – it is impossible to know if this is true. For less money, businesses can also advertise elsewhere and have text-only sponsored links.

MySpace pages

These are a free and easy way to display information about products and services and to communicate with the target audience. MySpace pages including a messaging space by default, and are highly customizable.

For businesses whose products or services are not aimed at the MySpace demographic, conducting a MySpace advertising campaign or creating a MySpace profile may well not be worth the effort – there is a notable lack of professional firms with MySpace pages, for example. It all depends on your target audience at the end of the day.

BEBO
(http://www.bebo.com)

Although in overall user numbers, Bebo falls behind MySpace and Facebook, Bebo is the largest of the three in the UK. With an easy-to-use and easy-on-the-eye interface, Bebo is a pleasure to use. In terms of functionality, Bebo is very similar to MySpace. Bebo users can:

- have their own pages on which to display their profiles;

- chat with other users on their own pages;

- make other Bebo members their 'friends';

- keep a blog;

- upload photos;

- upload videos – a very similar service to that provided by YouTube (discussed later);

- add various 'widgets' to their profile pages – widgets are the equivalent of applications on Facebook and are mostly for entertainment (for example, virtual pets).

Like MySpace, Bebo includes a section for music, on which bands can publish information about themselves and chat with fans. It has an equivalent section for authors. Also, like MySpace, Bebo offers businesses the opportunity to advertise in various spaces across the site; also like MySpace, these spaces are not cheap.

Bebo is a service aimed at those in school, college or university, and is designed purely for social networking. It is not suitable for professional networking. Whilst the same could be said of Facebook, the difference with Facebook is that although it is designed for social use, the site does have professional and business users, so it has now gone beyond the purely social. Bebo's users generally young – school or university age and not much beyond that.

Our view on Bebo from a business perspective, is that, as with MySpace, it is only relevant to those businesses whose target audience coincides with the Bebo demographic. The only other type of business that Bebo could appeal to is authors who are targeting a teenage/young adult audience. In other words, Bebo is relevant to the following types of business:

- musicians

- authors

- other businesses selling products/services to young people

TWITTER
(http://www.twitter.com)

Whilst other social networking services seem to get more and more complex, Twitter is simple in terms of what it does but complicated to explain. As of May 2008, Twitdir (http://twitdir.com/) estimated that there were 1.5 million Twitter users. Whilst it is nowhere near as popular as contemporaries such as Facebook or MySpace, Twitter is a big online player.

Twitter is often described as a 'micro-blog'. The service asks its users only one question: 'What are you doing?' Its users have just 140 characters in which to express themselves; the service is not a full blog, does not offer podcast or video facilities, or anything else for that matter. Remarkably, Twitter has become a big success in the online social and professional networking arena, at least in part because of this simplicity.

Whilst the means of contributing to Twitter may be simple and restricted, the means of interaction are diverse. First, let's look at interacting with others. With Twitter, you 'follow' people, provided of course that they want you to follow them. This means that Twitter will show you the latest 'tweets' (a Twitter message) from those that you 'follow'. Because everyone else can do the same, this leads to groups of friends on Twitter having big open conversations. In terms of that interaction, as well as just writing statements, users can direct comments at specific people (using an '@[username]' format) and can include links to websites in their tweets.

Second, there are various different methods of interaction. Whilst some people access Twitter through the 'traditional route' – the website http://www.twitter.com – there are other ways available: by text message from your mobile phone; by accessing the Twitter mobile service if your phone has internet access. The latter method is used by many who use Twitter whilst on the move. As well as there being various technological means of accessing Twitter, Twitter communications are also popping up all over the place. This is because Twitter has opened up its interface to programmers, allowing them to develop widgets that, for example, show Twitter feeds on blogs and websites.

So, is Twitter useful for businesses? For some types of business and businesspeople, the answer already is a clear 'yes'. As you'd predict, a lot of Twitter-using business-types to date have been in the technology and online sectors. For example, Michael Arrington of popular technology blog Techcrunch has commented:

> [Twitter] is now an important part of my work and social life, as I carry on bite-sized conversations with thousands of people around the world throughout the day. It's a huge marketing tool, and information tool. But it is also a social habit that's hard to kick.[2]

Some parts of the media are also incorporating Twitter into their online offerings. For example, UK newspaper *The Guardian* (http://www.guardian.co.uk) provides a Twitter feed for its technology section. Another UK example, the BBC News website (http://news.bbc.co.uk/), provides Twitter news updates. Within the technology industry, computer company Dell encourages its employees to use Twitter to talk about the company.

Whilst Twitter's user base and those that have used it for business to date have their roots firmly in the technology industry, the types of business and people who might make profitable or productive use of Twitter are likely to be wider than that. Any business with an online presence may find that a Twitter presence complements their online offering, including those who have concluded after reading the first part of our book that operating a blog is not for them.

Consumer-content Distribution Sites

YOUTUBE
(www.youtube.com)

YouTube is a massively popular video sharing website. It was launched in February 2005 and in the short time since then, the world has witnessed and participated in YouTube's meteoric rise. In August 2006, the *Wall Street Journal* reported that at that time there were 5.1 million videos, which had been viewed 1.73 billion times, and took up 45 terabytes of storage space (http://online.wsj.com/

---

2   Michael Arrington (2008) 'Twitter May Not Have to Care about Uptime Any Longer', TechCrunch, 22 April, http://www.techcrunch.com/2008/04/22/twitter-may-not-have-to-care-about-uptime-any-longer/.

public/article/SB115689298168048904-5wWyrSwyn6RfVfz9NwLk774VUWc_
20070829.html?mod=rss_free). As well as receiving popular acclaim, YouTube
has also been a hit with the media. For example, *PC World Magazine* named
YouTube the ninth best product of 2006.

YouTube is well-known for having significant copyright-infringement
issues. These issues arise because many of the videos that users upload are
extracts from television shows and films. It has been sued a number of times,
and as a result has entered into licensing agreements with various major
copyright owners (such as companies in the television and music industries)
to avoid further issues.

Like MySpace, the site is perceived to be used predominately by teenagers
and young adults. For this demographic, YouTube has even been said to be a
direct competitor to television as an entertainment medium.

The type of videos featured on YouTube reflect its young demographic;
there are few videos of interest to a business audience. There are a few such
videos, and the viewing figures for these suggest that placing promotional or
informative videos on YouTube could be a worthwhile means of publicity. Here
are a few examples at the time of writing:

- 'How to Create a Successful E-Commerce Website', uploaded by
  allbusinessdotcom. This had been viewed 954 times in the three
  months that it had been on the site and 12 people considered it a
  'favourite'.

- 'The Best Way to Hire Employees', also from allbusinessdotcom
  had been viewed 1264 times and was a favourite of six people.

- 'Marketing in Films and TV' by ProductIntegration had been
  viewed 94 times but was not anyone's favourite.

YouTube gives its users and audience a variety of features. Users can join groups
with interests in particular video subjects. Videos on the site can be embedded
into other social media, such as blogs and MySpace. Users can comment on
videos and can even upload vidoed 'responses' to videos, so one video can
result in many connected videos. There is a messaging facility allowing users
to communicate with each other privately. Users get individual pages on the
site, featuring all of their videos and including a space where others can make
comments about them and their videos. All this makes YouTube an exciting
and entertaining website.

In terms of business opportunities, like MySpace, the main opportunity is for those with products and services aimed at the teenage and young adult market. Advertising does not come cheap on YouTube; the site asks potential advertisers: 'Do you have a campaign budget of at least $25,000?' This is not an advertising opportunity for small businesses. At the time of writing, the site contains the following types of adverts:

- a cable television company

- a mobile phone company

- hotel and holiday companies

- personalized car registration plates

- car insurance.

There are a number of business groups on YouTube, although at the time of writing they had only a small number of members – the largest business group we found had seven members. Because of the low membership, these business groups did not appear to present any major networking opportunities.

The other opportunity comes from uploading videos relevant to your business audience, and publicizing such videos on your blog or on other forms of social media. Using this kind of publicity, the 'How to Create a Successful E-Commerce Website' video mentioned above had been viewed almost 1 000 times. How to create and publish videos online is part of the wider subject of videocasting, which we discuss in Chapter 11.

FLICKR
(http://flickr.com/)

Flickr is the photo-equivalent to YouTube, and the online home of the photography enthusiast. It allows users to upload, manage, share and view photos. Photos can be made available either to the entire world or restricted to friends and/or family. Users can choose to call specific Flickr users 'friends' or simply 'contacts', depending on the level of access they want to give to their photos. Photos can be put into 'albums' and can be uploaded to one of the many thousands of photography groups on the site. The photography groups often contain thousands of photos, and numerous discussions between group members.

Flickr was launched in February 2004 and its user-base has expanded rapidly. Whilst Flickr does not release details of its user base, various estimates by commentators made in 2006–07 put the total at between 19 million and 23 million. In November 2007, Techcrunch reported that Flickr users had uploaded over 2 billion photos to the site.[3] Flickr was purchased by Yahoo! in March 2005 for an undisclosed sum.

Unlike the social media services discussed so far, Flickr is not an entirely free-of-charge service. Or at least, if you want to use the service for free, your ability to upload photos is significantly restricted. Probably because it is aimed at hobbyists, this has not stopped Flickr from becoming popular; there are a significant number of subscribers to the site. According to Flickr, the site has over 7 million registered users, although its owner Yahoo! is unwilling to specify how many of those are fee-paying users.

The social networking on Flickr has translated into meeting in person on a number of occasions. Certain groups – typically those based in a specific geographic location – will have meetings or go on photography walks.

Flickr was one of the first websites to be described as 'Web 2.0' because it is incredibly easy and versatile to use. In terms of putting photos into the website, users can upload:

- from a computer using the website itself or specially created uploading software (very useful for bulk uploads);

- from mobile devices that have internet connections.

Once uploaded, Flickr creates a number of versions of the photo in different sizes, so that users can easily download an appropriately sized photo. Flickr allows users to do various things with the photos:

- Tag them, so that they are viewable by tags. For example, this allows a user to view all photos (by themselves or by the Flickr community as a whole) with the tag 'nature'.

- Geotag them, so that they are viewable by the location in which they were taken. For example, this allows a user to view all photos (by themselves, the whole Flickr community, or a specific Flickr group) that were taken in Southampton, UK.

---

3   Michael Arrington (2007) '2 Billion Photos on Flickr', TechCrunch, 13 November, http://www. techcrunch.com/2007/11/13/2-billion-photos-on-flickr/.

- Place the photos on blogs and websites.

- Organize them into 'albums'.

In addition, other users can do the following:

- Comment on photos. This can lead to long threads of comments for particularly popular photos.

- Call photos 'favourites'.

Unlike YouTube, Flickr does not appear to have any major issues with copyright infringement. When we asked about the number of copyright infringement complaints or claims Flickr receives, Yahoo! refused to give a statement. However, from the author's personal experience as a Flickr user, the vast majority of publicly available Flickr photographs appear to be original in the sense that they were taken by Flickr users. Maybe this PR silence is Flickr's strategy for stopping claims!

Flickr is strictly not for commercial use and is very definite on this issue. To quote the Flickr community guidelines (http://www.flickr.com/guidelines. gne):

Flickr is for personal use only. If you sell products, services or yourself through your photostream, we will terminate your account. Any other commercial use of Flickr, Flickr technologies (including APIs, Flickrmail, etc), or Flickr accounts must be approved by Flickr.

For the average business without a large advertising budget, there are therefore no commercial opportunities to be gained from the site, other than using the site as a storage place for the photos you use on your blog. This does not mean that Flickr is not a valuable resource for the business user, however; Flickr is an example of well-executed social media. Use or browsing of the site allows you to gain a good understanding of what social media sites are all about.

For the business with a large advertising budget who is interested in the Flickr demographic, there does, however, appear to be some opportunity to market using Flickr. For example, in March 2007, the technology company HP created and sponsored a Flickr group called 'HP Resolutionaries' as part of its marketing campaign 'Resolution: An Artists View'. When viewed on 15

March 2007, the group had 483 members, who in total had shared over 1479 of their photos. The marketing campaign was to mark the launch of an HP photo printer. This is a good example of where a marketing campaign has been able to directly communicate with its target audience – digital photographers – through social media. Although the cost of sponsoring a Flickr group is something that Flickr keeps to itself, it's safe to say that this is likely to be beyond the marketing budget of most small businesses.

Virtual Worlds

Virtual worlds have existed on the internet for many years now. The 3D worlds used by the likes of Second Life, which we discuss below, are the latest development, but such worlds have been in existence since less-glamorous days when the internet was text-only. From being text-only, other worlds began to appear that used 2D graphics to represent characters and people. The 3D variety is fairly commonplace, and looks set to get more commonplace in future years.

SECOND LIFE

Second Life is probably the most well-known virtual online world. Information from its creator, Linden Labs, and from news stories, paints an impressive picture. Linden Lab's website claims that the world has a population of 6 123 723 and a capitalist economy that trades the equivalent of millions of US dollars each month.

Residents of the world can do pretty much whatever they want. They have the ability to create objects of varying complexity, from clothes to cars, and own the intellectual property (IP) rights in these objects. They can rent land and create buildings on that land. They can do a lot of things that people do in real life, such as shop, go to nightclubs and even run businesses. They can look pretty much how they want to look – in Second Life, you're likely to find yourself interacting with cybergoths and squirrels, amongst other things.

Linden Labs has spent $8 million over three years on Second Life since it launched in 2003. Linden Labs wants to recover this investment, and so whilst you can use Second Life for free as a 'basic user', with this set-up you will not receive any money to spend in the world (unless you pay Linden Labs via a 'currency exchange') and do not have the ability to buy land. To achieve anything meaningful as a business will therefore come at a price. For example:

- You will have to sign up as premium user to get the ability to buy land. Linden Labs also gives you a 'weekly stipend' of Linden dollars to 'live' on. You pay $9.95 per month to be a premium user.

- To own land, you must buy it first. You then also pay a monthly land use fee for the privilege of owning that land.

This virtual world of freedom and commerce has generated a lot of hype and a lot of interest from 'real-life' businesses. Reuters, the news agency, has an office in the world and has a journalist stationed there who covers events within the world. Cisco, the IT company, has representatives in Second Life who are there to communicate with Cisco customers. Other large technology companies have a presence in Second Life: Sun Microsystems, Dell, IBM.

In addition to these technology companies, a large London-based law firm, Field Fisher Waterhouse, has recently established an office in Second Life. The firm announced its Second Life presence on 23 April 2007. The move was headed by David Naylor, a technology partner. In the firm's press release, David set out the reasoning behind the move:

> Virtual worlds offer a compelling environment for communication and collaboration, as well as an important commercial distribution channel. By establishing a Second Life presence, we're able to interact in new and engaging ways with our clients and the wider community. Businesses are moving increasingly rapidly into Second Life and other 3D internet environments and their advisers should be there with them.[4]

In an article in the Law section of UK newspaper *The Times*, Naylor added that the companies doing business in Second Life needed legal advice, and that with major companies already present in Second Life, he hoped that Field Fisher Waterhouse's presence there would attract them as clients.[5]

We interviewed David Naylor of Field Fisher Waterhouse about the firm's experiences of running a law office in Second Life.

---

4   Field Fisher Waterhouse (2007) 'Field Fisher Waterhouse is first major law firm to launch Second Life presence', 23 April, http://www.ffw.com/news/2007/apr/field-fisher-waterhouse-is-fir.aspx.
5   Michael Herman and Alex Spence (2007) 'First UK law firm opens "virtual" office in Second Life', *The Times*, 24 April, http://business.timesonline.co.uk/tol/business/law/article1699474.ece.

FIELD FISHER WATERHOUSE AND SECOND LIFE

What was involved in setting up your Second Life office

Our offices were built and developed by Depo Consulting and we worked closely with them on the internal fit out. This involved working alongside them to come up with a design that reflected the firm's branding and putting together information about the firm from brochures, the website and press coverage to include inside the offices. We also currently have an art exhibition on our upper ground floor. This is all an ongoing process and we are gradually adding more and more to the interior, particularly now we have taken advice from the consultants and are able to add to and update our Second Life offices ourselves.

What sort of presence do you maintain there?

We have a team of seven (a combination of lawyers and support staff), whose avatars staff the offices, greeting visitors and providing them with information they may request. With the whole team involved we try to ensure the offices are staffed as much as possible, but we currently leave this to each individual to fit in with their other work commitments. Of course, having representation in our offices doesn't prevent the Second Life team from getting on with other work. We all have a second PC with access to Second Life and go in when we get the time. It is possible to have Second Life running and be alerted when someone comes into our offices. This way we can fit this in as part of our working day.

Apart from massive publicity, what have you got out of being in Second Life so far? For example, has it led to any new clients or additional work from current clients?

Since opening our office on Second Life we have had thousands of visitors. They range from existing and potential clients (real life and Second Life!), potential recruits (legal and professional services), journalists, conference organizers, legal and other academics, other professional services businesses, and representatives of Second Life networking organizations.

Our primary reasons for establishing a presence were the communication and collaboration opportunities (we have used our premises to provide in-world seminars, and host very many meetings), and a desire to learn more about the environment and how people and businesses interact and trade in-world (and into the real world). We don't think any firm could properly expect to advise clients on virtual worlds legal issues without having a real understanding of the environment.

We also don't just think about Second Life in terms of what we can get out of it. We also see it as providing an opportunity to contribute. For example, we are exhibiting the works of a local artist in our art gallery, and we're also working with a charity that we support to provide them with some space and coverage in our offices and the business park that we have located in.

Of course, our involvement and work on virtual worlds matters has generated enquiries from our clients and contacts (mainly major corporations and brands) about setting up in Second Life and the legal and commercial issues they will need to understand and address to operate Second Life focused businesses. These issues range from in-world commerce and commercial contracting, intellectual property licensing and protection, privacy, employment and tax – so there is plenty for businesses to get to grips with. We are currently working on Second Life developer arrangements, and providing assistance to some in-world businesses on commercial and IP matters.

If your target market is the technology sector, a presence in Second Life is an obvious move. For professional services firms, it is less clear whether Second Life is worth the time and effort. The Intellectual Property and Technology team at UK law firm Freeth Cartwright LLP also considered establishing itself in Second Life during 2006/7 and decided against it, giving the following key reasons:

- Second Life presented no obvious business opportunities for the firm. With Linden Labs enforcing IP rights within the world, a key role was removed.

- To have a real presence within the world, the firm would have had to allocate someone to be there during every working day of the week. Without any obvious business opportunity with which to cover the cost of this, a presence was difficult to justify.

- There were various technical issues, such as Second Life operating very slowly, crashing regularly, and the difficulty of making Second Life operate from behind a firewall.

The point about the time investment is something we regard as being a key difference between operating in a virtual online world and some of the other social media we have seen. Whereas with a technology such as a blog or a social networking site you can log in and out, make and respond to communications as and when you have the time, with a virtual world you must by definition spend time there to communicate and interact. Of course, if you can justify this time investment by the return you will get in new business from that virtual world, this is not an issue.

Wikis

CHAPTER

9

A wiki is a type of website that allows its users to add, remove, and otherwise edit and change the content of the website. This ability to edit by multiple persons makes wikis a very effective tool for know-how management and collaborative authoring.

A short online video explaining wikis has been produced by Common Craft (http://www.commoncraft.com/video-wikis-plain-english).

The nature of wikis and their use is best explained by looking at Wikipedia, the most popular wiki in the world.

Wikipedia
(http://www.wikipedia.org)

Wikipedia is a free online encyclopedia. It was written by, and is still being written by, its users. Today, Wikipedia is one of the most popular websites in the world.

The Wikipedia project was launched in January 2001, and is operated by the Wikimedia Foundation, a not-for-profit organization. Although originally an English language project, Wikipedia is now available in over 250 languages, although the amount of content varies from language to language; only 18 have more than 50 000 articles. Across all languages, at the time of writing Wikipedia had just under 8 million articles, of which 1.9 million were in English.

There have been controversies over Wikipedia's reliability and accuracy, with many critics taking the view that its authorship by 'amateurs' would lead to poor quality articles and inconsistent coverage of subject matters. Whilst these sort of accusations have never gone away, a 2005 analysis of Wikipedia and *Encyclopaedia Britannica* has helped bolster Wikipedia's reputation as a reliable information source. The analysis, by the science journal *Nature*, of 42 articles from each encylopaedia, found that major errors in Wikipedia were the exception rather than the rule, and that the encyclopaedias contained roughly the same number of errors (http://www.nature.com/news/2005/051212/full/438900a.html). Other controversies about Wikipedia come and go; at the time of writing, the current controversy was the editing of certain articles by government agencies and companies to remove information damaging to them.

Regardless of such issues, Wikipedia has established itself as a good first port of call when researching a particular subject. It is not the definitive research tool and probably never will be, but is a good starting point and a brilliant example of what collaboration can create.

HOW WIKIPEDIA WORKS

All the articles on Wikipedia have been created by individuals, and most have been edited by at least one other person. With a few exceptions (particularly for articles on controversial subjects or people), anyone can edit an article on Wikipedia.

Wikipedia is very well established, and over time an infrastructure of rules and procedures has developed. There are various rules about the content of articles, a key one being that facts must be backed by a citation to another source. A hierarchy has also developed, with contributors able to become editors – with more control over articles – at the approval of existing editors, and even a 'judicial committee' with the ability to decide on issues that editors have been unable to resolve.

Wikipedia is probably the most advanced wiki in terms its community and community rules, but the wiki software powering it can be used by anyone wanting to set up a wiki. The sections that follow describe where wikis fit into the overall picture, how businesses can benefit from wikis and the wiki software and services available.

WIKIS VS. BLOGS

If wikis and blogs allow people to discuss subjects matters online, why have both become established? Why hasn't one or the other faded away? The reason is that, whilst both share in common the function of allowing people to discuss things online, wikis and blogs are quite different.

The key differences between the two are:

1.   the degree of control possessed by a wiki creator compared to a blogger; and

2.   the 'voice' of wikis compared with blogs.

Blogs are a means for one person or organization to communicate with the outside world. A blog may receive comments from its audience and discussions may happen on the blog as a result of these comments, but ultimately the blog is projecting the voice of the person or organization that controls it. With wikis, on the other hand, the content and 'voice' are built from the contributions made by the various people using the wiki, and the person/organization that set the wiki up has less control over those contributions. (Of course, a particular wiki may be perceived as having a particular bias or focus [for example, Wikipedia is often accused of having a liberal bias], and the creator of the wiki can restrict access to and/or have the power to edit the wiki to a select group.)

As tools, blogs are not 'better' than wikis; they are different tools. We now look at some of the uses to which businesses can put wikis. It is worth noting that you would struggle to get these uses out of a blog.

How Businesses Can Make Use of Wikis

The wiki that we have discussed so far, Wikipedia, is a public wiki. Most businesses wikis are not public; they are private and only accessible within a particular organization.

Businesses mainly use wikis for information and know-how management. Because a wiki is a tool that allows anyone to contribute, wikis are an excellent way to record knowledge held by various people within an organization. They are equally good at making that information available to all. An organization does not need to install special software so that employees can read a wiki; it will be viewable using a web browser (for example, Internet Explorer) that employees will have installed and be familiar with already. Where a wiki is being used in place of an office application such as a word processor, it is worth noting that an online office application (discussed in the next section) may be better for the task than a wiki.

There are numerous examples of businesses using wikis as effective knowledge management tools. One is the bank Dresdner Kleinwort Wasser (DKW). According to the stories of wiki success contained on the Wiki software website Socialtext (http://www.socialtext.com), DKW has been using wikis since 1997. Whilst wikis were initially used mainly by the bank's IT staff, in 2004 it implemented an internal wiki for use throughout the organization. Amongst other things, DKW staff use the wiki for recording and allowing people to add to training materials, writing agendas for internal meetings, developing ideas and generally recording information that would otherwise have been kept all over the place on individual computers and different office applications and document management facilities. Another user is Nokia, which has a private wiki for recording and managing product development information (http://twiki.org/cgi-bin/view/Main/TWikiSuccessStoryOfYahoo).

This ability to easily manage information within an organization can of course be extended to projects involving multiple organizations. As any commercial lawyer will know, distributing and keeping under control multiple versions of documents that are circulating during the negotiation of a deal can turn into a nightmare. On a large deal, each party will have various people responsible for various parts of that deal – both within the law firms acting on the deal and within each client organization. It is very easy to miss people out of the distribution list when emailing the latest draft of the contract documents; the people involved will also be under strain from the number of emails discussing aspects of the deal.

A secure private wiki accessible on the internet could be set up in place of the contract documents; some wikis even allow you to directly import the contents of a word-processor document. This wiki could then be accessed and edited by the various people on the deal. A good wiki package will keep track of the edits, so that you can see the various amendments made by people. The two key advantages of this approach, as compared to the traditional document-circulation route, are:

- Everyone can see and be certain of the latest version of the document. There is no risk of confusion over what is the latest version and of mistakenly editing an out-of-date document (not something that brings you great popularity with those who then have to work out how your changes fit in with the latest version!).

- Email traffic is substantially reduced, or even eliminated.

The sheer flexibility of wikis as a way of collaborating, collecting and managing information means that their potential as a business tool potentially goes even further; the examples and benefits set out above are just the tip of the iceberg. Next time you start a project, set up a wiki for the project and get everyone using it. You are unlikely to regret it, and will probably be reluctant to use the traditional method once you've used a wiki.

Wiki Products

There are a large number of wiki products available. What is best for you depends upon a number of factors:

- whether you want a commercial product or a free-of-charge open source product;

- whether you want to host the wiki or have someone else do this for you;

- your level of technical knowledge.

Generally speaking, using a commercial product will mean that the product supplier does the hosting for you, you have support available and you don't need any technical knowledge. Using an open source product means you will get the product free, you will have more opportunity to customize the wiki, but in return you must invest more time in learning to use the product and will probably have to arrange for the hosting of the wiki. As far as the general user of the wiki is concerned, it probably will not matter whether the wiki is a commercial product or open source; both are generally quite easy to use.

Some examples of commercial and free wiki products are listed below.

COMMERCIAL WIKI PRODUCTS

- **Confluence** (http://www.atlassian.com/software/confluence): From software company Atlassian, this is the choice of many big businesses that have started using wikis. You can either host it or Atlassian will host it for you. Confluence is feature-filled and easy to use, but such functionality comes at a price. If you want to host it yourself, Confluence costs (at the time of writing) $1,200 per year for 25 users. After the first year, if you wish to keep receiving maintenance you must pay for this too. The hosted version costs $890 per year for 25 users, although maintenance is not an issue, or an additional cost, with this version.

- **Socialtext** (http://www.socialtext.com): A popular wiki for businesses from a 'wiki company' of the same name. Like Confluence, Socialtext has a lot of functionality and is easy to use, and you can either host it yourself or Socialtext will host it for you.

FREE WIKI PRODUCTS

- **PBWiki** (http://www.pbwiki.com): This is the wiki used by the authors of this book. PBWiki hosts your wiki, unlike a lot of the free products. From our experience, this wiki is easy to use (the PB part of the name stands for 'peanut butter', because PBwiki, Inc. believes that using the wiki is as easy as making a peanut butter sandwich.)

- **SnipSnap** (http://www.snipsnap.org): A combined wiki and blog. Like PBWiki, SnipSnap hosts your wiki.

- **MediaWiki** (http://www.mediawiki.org): This is the wiki used for Wikipedia. MediaWiki's main role is to act as the software for Wikipedia, although you can download it and use it for your own wiki. Whilst the MediaWiki organization is not there to support users, there is a large amount of (largely technical) information about MediaWiki on the web, and a community of users there to help you.

Online Office
Applications

CHAPTER

10

In recent years, a new type of office package has emerged, namely the online office application. This means that office applications such as word processors and spreadsheets can be accessed online. These packages are often as easy to use as traditional software-based office applications, and are arguably easier to use because there's no installation or regular upgrades to be done by the user. All that is needed is a computer with a website browser.

In effect, online office applications are simply wikis that look like and work like office software. One benefit of online office applications compared with traditional wikis is that they are already familiar to most people, because they look like ordinary office software. Because of this, for collaborative projects involving people resistant to new technology, using an online office application may be a better option than using a wiki, even if a wiki platform is just as suited for the particular project.

Online office applications have an immediate advantage over their software counterparts: documents can be accessed anywhere with an internet connection. There is no need to email documents to yourself or carry them around on a memory stick, CD, or any other storage medium. What's more, the backup and storage facilities and processes of the application providers is in most cases going to be better than those of most users. Not many people remember to back up their documents regularly, whereas with an online application provider this is, or should be, part of their practices.

Online office applications hold documents privately and securely, meaning that using this method of storage and access should not be an issue for most organizations. In many ways, holding a document on such an application so that others can edit it is probably more secure than sending the same document by email.

Online office applications have huge potential as an aid to collaboration. With such applications, for the first time distribution of documents for a piece of work being done by multiple people is not an issue; no distribution needs to be done because the document is held in one place and accessible by all collaborators. In fact, some online applications let multiple people simultaneously edit a document! This combination of one document and easy access by all make online office applications a potentially powerful new way for businesses to work on projects.

At the time of writing, the main weaknesses of the online office applications available are:

- They lack of functionality compared with their software equivalents. For example, not many have sophisticated clause numbering or cross-referencing systems, so these applications are not going to be an option for contract negotiations or lengthy documents that need to look professional.

- There is little support from the application providers. The application providers generally do not provide contractual guarantees on issues such as dedicated customer support, service availability, backups or security. These issues are very important to organizations working on important projects.

Our view is that it can only be a matter of time before an online application arrives that addresses these problems; the potential market for online office applications is huge and ready for the taking. Below, we discuss two of the main online office applications available at the time of writing.

Google Docs and Spreadsheets

(http://docs.google.com)

As the name suggests, Google Docs and Spreadsheets provides an online word processor and spreadsheet. Whilst both are relatively basic, they are very easy to use, even simultaneously by multiple collaborators. Parts of this book were written using the Google word processor. The applications can be used free of charge; you simply need to sign up for a Google account.

Not only are the word processor and spreadsheet easy to use, but the overall system is very intuitive as well. Documents can be housed in a single folder and multiple folders, collaborators can be invited to access the documents by simply typing in their email addresses and documents can be easily saved to a computer in standard office file formats.

The word processor contains basic formatting tools, and a powerful compare function in the word processor allows you to easily see who has made what changes to what document versions.

The word processor operates in a standard website page, relying on the usual web page format, HTML. The big positive of this is that Google Docs will run efficiently in almost any web browser. The downside is that the documents you create may suffer occasional HTML-related hiccups. For example, when text is pasted from other word processors or from web pages, the text may bring HTML code with it. This is not a fault as such; the HTML is there to do such things as put the text in bold or italics, or make it use a particular font or font size. The difficulty can be removing the formatting in question; sometimes Google Docs does not remove the formatting in question as you deselect bold or italics from the menu, or choose another font type or font size. This issue should not be overplayed, however; it can be overcome with a bit of fiddling, and you do not need technical knowledge to do so.

The spreadsheet is relatively basic compared with commercial spreadsheet software such as Lotus 123 and Microsoft Excel. However, given that most business users are unlikely to need advanced accounting functionality, the Google spreadsheet does the job and does it well.

Whilst keeping documents privately by default, Google Docs lets you make them public or even publish them to websites.

Overall, Google Docs and Spreadsheets is an adequate replacement for standard office software for basic tasks, and its collaborative features are excellent.

Zoho
(http://www.zoho.com)

Zoho is a range of office applications, including:

- word processor
- spreadsheet

- database

- CRM (customer relations management)

- presentation creator

- calendar.

As with its Google competitor, these applications far more basic than their traditional software-based equivalents, but are fine for most day-to-day office tasks. Most of the applications are free of charge, although there are charges for the use of some applications, such as CRM, beyond set limits. Overall, considering that there is such a range and they are free, the applications are good in terms of features.

Like Google Docs, Zoho runs in a standard HTML website page, so it can run in most browsers and without installing any extra software on your computer. As with Google Docs, the side-effect of running in HTML is that your documents can occasionally run into HTML-connected difficulties.

At the time of writing, our view was that the Google word processor and spreadsheet were easier to use than the Zoho equivalents. Google's collaborative features, such as how someone gets access to a document after they have been invited to edit it by an existing user, were more intuitive and easy to use than those in Zoho.

However, the sheer application range is impressive and worth considering next time you are involved in something collaborative. If you can't do it in Google Docs, chances are you can in Zoho, provided you put in some effort!

Adobe Buzzword

Buzzword is an online word processor brought to us by Adobe, the company behind Flash, the media player. Flash is used on many of the most popular websites. Rather than go for the standard website page approach used by Google Docs and Zoho, Buzzword uses Adobe's own Flash technology as its platform. This has resulted in an easy-to-use product with a smart interface and a neat look. It also means, of course, that, unlike the online office packages we've discussed so far, to use Buzzword you do not just need a website browser; you also need to install Flash.

Not being a built on simple website pages, Buzzword documents are less likely to suffer the kind of formatting glitches experienced in its competitors. However, the downside is that you need a higher-specification computer to run Buzzword; not every computer you use is going to have Flash installed. Accessibility is another issue raised by Buzzword; Flash-based products tend to be less easy to access and use by those with disabilities (such as visual impairment) than simple website pages. For example, accessibility software (such as text-to-speech readers) can encounter problems with Flash. However, Flash does allow products to include accessibility-enhancing features, and so it may be that Buzzword is usable by those with disabilities. At the time of writing, no accessibility report on Buzzword was available; there may be one available by the time you read this. Before installing Buzzword, it is therefore worth checking out whether Buzzword has accessibility issues.

Buzzword has powerful collaboration features allowing you to let multiple people view and edit a document. The sharing features are as easy to use as those in Google Docs.

What About Microsoft?

Anyone who knows even a little about the IT industry will tell you that when a technology bandwagon with 'mass market' written all over it starts rolling, Microsoft is the first to jump on board. This even happened with the internet itself; Microsoft only made serious investments into website browsers, in the form of Internet Explorer, after such software had become popular. Microsoft has been in the (offline) office software market since 1989. With the emergence of a huge potential market for online office applications, what has Microsoft been doing?

Microsoft provides two (offline) office software packages: the feature-intense Office and the relatively basic Works. Works is the first of the two packages that Microsoft is taking online. In late 2006, Microsoft announced plans to release an online version of Works, with the product subsidized by online advertising. The online version had not yet been released at the time of writing, and seems unlikely to be available until after this book has been published. Microsoft Works offers approximately the same level of features as those seen in the office packages we've discussed above; Microsoft's decision to take Works online before Office is therefore perhaps unsurprising.

From the indications given so far, the company's plans for taking Office online will lead to a different offering from those given by the online office packages discussed so far. In late 2007, Microsoft announced the launch of Office Live Workspace (OLW). The company said that this would not be an online version of the package; it is an online storage area for existing users of Office 2003 and 2007.

In terms of collaborative working, OLW is not looking like a viable option for all users. Taking the example of a collaborative project that involves a group of people working on a document, if all the people in your project group have copies of Office installed on their computers, you can use OLW to store a document and the entire group will be able to work on the document. On the other hand, if someone in your project group does not have Office installed, whilst they can log in to OLW to view the document and add comments about the document, they are not be able to edit the document itself. They are effectively excluded from the collaboration. What's more, an existing Office user will be unable to work on the document if they happen to use someone else's computer to access OLW, if that computer:

- has an office suite other than Microsoft Office;

- has Office installed, but not the correct version; or

- has the correct version of Word installed but does not have OLW set up.

Whilst OLW might be great for collaborative working in a situation where everyone is guaranteed to have Office 2003 or 2007, for example a project within a single organization, it seems that OLW will be no use for any other scenario.

Podcasting and Videocasting

CHAPTER

11

Podcasting

Podcasting is a form of distribution of sound recordings over the internet. Whilst many audio-files are now called 'podcasts' by their creators, a podcast is generally understood to mean an audio-file with an RSS feed attached (RSS feeds are discussed in Chapter 1). The existence of the RSS feed means that podcasts can be picked up by RSS readers. We mention a few websites that are podcast directories, and at core all these do is display RSS feeds for audio-files.

Whilst podcasts can be played using standard music playing software such as Windows Media Player, the use of podcasting software is what makes podcasts so much more useful – from an information perspective – than standard sound files. If, using podcasting software, you subscribe to podcasts from a certain source, you will be alerted to future podcasts from that source.

'Podcast' is a generic term and not derived from the Apple iPod; 'pod' stands for 'playable on demand'. There are two types of podcast. The first is the downloaded podcast: the podcast will be stored as an audio-file on your computer for you to listen to when you want and with flexibility as to how you listen to it – on your computer or on audio-file-compatible devices such as portable digital music players that you can take anywhere. The second is the streaming podcast: with this type, you do not receive an audio-file; the podcast is gradually 'streamed' to your computer so that you can listen to it whilst connected to the internet, but you do not end up with an audio-file to keep.

A common type of podcast is the internet 'radio station'. With podcast creation software, anyone can create an online radio station, issuing 'shows' that anyone with an internet connection can find and subscribe to. Most podcasts to date fall broadly into the 'personal interest' category. For example, at the time of writing, the Podcast Alley directory of podcasts (http://www.podcastalley.com), featured 6 000+ music podcasts, 2 500+ comedy podcasts and thousands of 'personal interest' podcasts (technology, health, spirituality, TV and film). On the other hand, the directory featured just over 1500 'business' podcasts, a number dwarfed by the other categories. This reflects the hobbyist origins of podcasting.

Podcasting has the potential to become a very important and useful communications medium for businesses, including for their advisors. The written word is just one form of communicating information, and for a lot of people it is not the top choice. Listening to someone explain a concept or issue can be a lot more effective than reading a written explanation. Some people just prefer it, hence the popularity of audio books.

BUSINESS PODCASTING

Most business podcasts available are by:

- businesses, either giving general information on a subject as a way of raising their profile or discussing a specific product/service;

- media businesses, distributing the podcasts as a means of getting visitors and hence advertising revenue from site visits and the podcasts themselves.

An example is SmallBizPod (http://www.smallbizpod.co.uk), which contains hundreds of podcasts relevant to small businesses, such as how to import goods. The podcasts are in a radio show format, with a presenter interviewing experts on subjects as well as business people generally. For those interviewed, SmallBizPod is an excellent way of raising their profile and attracting customers. One company using podcasts to reach its market is the technology outfit Verizon. Verizon has published podcasts covering a variety of subjects relevant to companies with IT needs (www.podtech.net/home/feed/?&category_name= verizon+business&feed-type=mp3&subscription-id=10000).

Even law firms have begun to experiment with podcasts. OUT-LAW.com, the IT law website run by UK firm Pinsent Masons, is an excellent example of how a law firm can use social media to raise its profile and bring in legal work generally. As well as general legal information and stories in written form, the site features OUT-LAW Radio, a weekly 10-minute podcast (http://www.out-law.com/page-7212). The podcasts feature stories and interviews on the topical IT law issues and discussions on technology developments generally.

We interviewed Struan Robertson, editor of the OUT-LAW.com legal news website, about the OUT-LAW Radio series of podcasts.

OUT-LAW RADIO

Why did you decide to start podcasting as an addition to your written-word output?

We had three reasons for getting into podcasting. The first was purely editorial: we thought it would add to our coverage of technology law to produce radio-style content as well as written content. We think it adds tremendously to the vitality of our coverage to allow people to hear the actual participants in stories talk about them, rather than just read their words in stories. It also allows us to cover stories in a different way, in a more relaxed features style and in more depth.

Secondly, we felt that podcasting is a great match for our audience, who are busy professional people who are likely to be technologically literate. We felt if we could give them material in a format that they could take anywhere on a digital audio device – in the car or on the train while commuting, for example – and if we could do it in an enjoyable, accessible style, then that would be something they would want.

Thirdly, we felt that given that the law firm's lawyers are advising on new media issues, on the legal side of the development and production of new media products, it would deepen the firm's understanding of the issues involved if OUT-LAW actually produced multi-media content.

When did you first begin podcasting?

In August 2007.

Who do you involve in OUT-LAW Radio?

OUT-LAW Radio is produced by one journalist, Matthew Magee, and overseen by an editor, Struan Robertson. We call on the expertise of Pinsent Mason's lawyers for comment on many of the issues we cover.

What software and equipment do you use?

We record with a BeyerDynamic M58 microphone into a mini disc recorder for mobile recording (later feeding that into a PC), and with a telephone recording connector directly into the PC for phone calls.

We use Cubase as a recording and editing system with a Lexicon Lambda breakout box for audio inputs into a standard PC. Because the version of Cubase we have does not output in mp3 format, we use the open source system Audacity to convert wav files into mp3s.

How long does it take to put together a typical podcast?

This is a tough question: some take calls to chase people over the course of weeks, some come together easily. The journalism side of chasing people happens over the course of about a fortnight and the actual production once all the interviews are in takes about six hours. In all, each 10-minute edition probably takes a day and a half to produce.

How many listeners do you have?

We don't publish listener numbers, but we have had a good conversion rate from our total audience into listeners (our audience is pretty highly specialized). The listenership was almost immediately at the level we had hoped for, and has risen since, though not dramatically.

What feedback have you received about your podcasts?

The feedback has been fantastic, and OUT-LAW Radio has been praised on a number of blogs. People have been shocked that the podcast actually sounds professional, since they are perhaps more used to podcasts that are simply recordings of entire conversations rather than edited, created programmes. People have appreciated particularly that we keep a very tight control of the length of the podcast, keeping it always between 10 and 12 minutes long.

What tips do you have for those thinking of podcasting?

The most important factor is: will your audience actually download and listen to podcasts? If yours is not a technically literate audience or is one that is already well served by the traditional broadcast media, you might want to think again before pouring resources into podcasting.

Another important thing to bear in mind is that a podcast should be journalism: it should be produced, not just allowed to happen. There is a reason that television and radio shows have teams of producers working on them: you need to apply proper editorial controls on the product. You need to chase down the right interviewees, have a definite idea of what you want to ask them, and you need to choose and use only the best answers. You need to weave all the interviews you have into a comprehensible and compelling story that your audience wants to hear, using the interviews to illuminate and expand on a strong narrative.

Many podcasts are too long and too lax. We feel strongly that just because there is no limit on the length a podcast can be, we shouldn't relax normal editorial discipline in telling the story in a punchy, concise way.

HOW TO GET AND LISTEN TO PODCASTS

Although your existing web browser will allow you to find podcasting sites and download podcasts, it is unlikely to let you subscribe to podcasts, losing much of the benefit of podcasts as a means of easily receiving information. You therefore need to install podcasting software. There is a variety of free podcast software available. Examples are:

- **iTunes** (http://www.apple.com/itunes): the computer software for Apple iPods, which allows you to search for and subscribe to podcasts.

- **Juice** (http://www.indiepodder.org for the directory, http://juicereceiver.sourceforge.net/ for the Juice software): A popular podcast application that was previously called iPodder and connected with the iPodder directory of podcasts.

Once you have installed your podcast software, you will be able to use it to search for and subscribe to podcasts. Some podcasting software integrates with your web browser, so you can subscribe to podcasts found whilst web surfing without having to switch applications.

HOW TO CREATE AND 'PUBLISH' A PODCAST

Because a podcast is just an audio-file with RSS feed information attached to it – or even just an audio-file on a website if you are not fussed about benefiting from RSS feeds – creating a podcast is relatively simple. You will need:

- an audio recorder;

- an audio editor to edit the sound recording – for example, you will probably want to ensure that the volume is right, and there may be parts of the recording that you want to rearrange or remove;

- somewhere to host the audio-file online;

- software to create and publish the RSS newsfeed for the audio-file.

Getting and using an audio recorder is relatively straightforward. Most operating systems come with audio-recording software installed, and there is a variety of recording software available online. Then all that you need is a microphone connected to the computer to make the recording. Many computers today come with a microphone installed, although to achieve good-quality sound it is often worth buying an external microphone. As an alternative, many mobile phones allow you to record a few minutes of audio, and then it is a case of transferring the audio-file to your computer (ways to transfer files from mobile phone to computer are discussed in the section on videocasting, below).

In terms of audio editors and RSS publishing software, there is a selection of commercial and free-of-charge software to choose from. For example:

- **Adobe Audition** (http://www.adobe.com/products/audition/index.html): A professional audio editing tool for Windows, and the successor to the well-respected CoolEdit. This is expensive, professional software and therefore designed for those who will be doing a lot of detailed audio editing, rather than the occasional podcaster. The UK retail price of £270–£300 + VAT at the time of writing reflects this.

- **Audacity** (http://audacity.sourceforge.net/): An open-source, free-of-charge sound editor for Windows and the Apple Mac. It is used by a lot of podcasters.

- **RecordForAll** (http://www.recordforall.com): A podcasting software bundle, which is an all-in-one podcast creator and publisher costing $70.

Next you need to upload the audio-file and, if possible, create an RSS newsfeed for it. If you are running a blog, your blogging service (particularly if you pay a fee for the service) will often allow you to upload files such as podcasts. There are also a number of podcast hosting services available. These include:

- **Switchpod** (http://www.switchpod.com): This hosting service can be used either free or, if you want more features and a greater monthly upload limit, for a fee. The service publicizes your podcast on its website. RSS newsfeeds are created automatically, allowing people to obtain the podcasts through RSS newsreaders.

- **Podcast FM** (http://www.podcastfm.co.uk): Another hosting service that can create RSS newsfeeds for you and can be used either free or, for more features and higher upload limits, for a charge.

- **RecordForAll** (http://www.recordforall.com): See above.

PLANNING A PODCAST

Planning a podcast is very much like planning any other presentation that you deliver: you must consider your target audience and how to keep the presentation interesting. Not many of us enjoy long monotonous lectures, so there is no reason why a similar format will work for podcasting. Two podcast structures stand out as being good for podcasting by professionals:

- **The interview**: You talk about your chosen subject – for example, an area of law or a recent deal that you have advised on – but with someone 'interviewing' you. This question-and-answer format works keeps things lively.

- **The radio show**: Two of the examples of podcasts that we have given use the radio show format. This means that the podcast can have different 'programmes' and probably feature some interviews.

Of course, not all podcasts need planning. If you are delivering a talk on a subject, recording the talk and turning it into a podcast means that the talk can be heard by a wider audience.

There are also ways to make a podcast stand out. Commonly used 'props' are music and sound effects. You can either licence in music to use, or choose from free-to-use music available on the internet. Before using a music or audio clip, it is worth doing some due diligence to ensure that it really is okay to use!

MAXIMIZING YOUR AUDIENCE FIGURES

Because podcasts are searchable on search engines such as Google, follow the search engine optimization (SEO) tips in Chapter 4 to increase your potential audience.

Videocasting

As the name suggests, videocasting is the video equivalent of podcasting. It is sometimes also referred to as 'vodcasting'. Like podcasts, videocasts are either in the form of video files that you download, or are streamed to your computer over the internet. To be considered a 'proper' videocast, listeners should be able to subscribe to the video using an RSS newsreader, just as you can with podcasts. Also like podcasts, videocasts are not just confined to computers; they can also be played on other types of media device such as portable media players and even some DVD players.

In all but the visual element of the video, there is very little difference in use or features between videocasts and podcasts. They are simply an alternative to text for delivering content. We will therefore focus on the practicalities.

HOW TO FIND AND VIEW VIDEOCASTS

Videocasts are available from many of the same sources as podcasts, such as iTunes and Indiepodder. There are also general video viewing sites such as YouTube.

HOW TO RECORD A VIDEOCAST: CHOOSING A CAMERA

Whilst there are videocasters that use professional recording equipment, for the occasional videocaster there is no need for this kind of expense. For the business videocaster, videocasting isn't about creating professional looking television; it is simply a means of getting information across and showing your personality at the same time.

For basic videocasts of three to ten minutes in duration, a camera-equipped mobile phone will be just fine, provided you have a means of getting the video on to a computer. Many camera-phones come with built-in video editing software, allowing you to cut the bits you don't want, leaving a decent enough video. In many ways, the videos produced by camera-phones are ideal for videocasting; they are small in size but of sufficient quality to be viewable. There are various ways to transfer the video on to a computer, depending on the phone and the computer:

- If your phone uses a memory card and your computer has a memory card reader, simply place the card into the reader and get the video file.

- Use the Bluetooth communications standard. Most phones have Bluetooth, and you can buy a Bluetooth reader for your computer for minimal expense.

- If you phone has infrared, you can buy a reader for your computer and transfer the video that way.

- If your phone is equipped with email, mail the video file to your computer email address.

Another means of recording a videocast is to buy a camera for your computer. These cameras plug into your computer and, as well as allowing you to record videocasts, have a variety of other applications such as video conferencing. Often, the cameras are no better quality than those used in mobile phones.

If you really want to show off, a digital video camera will allow you to create a high-resolution video and transfer this to your computer. It's worth reiterating the point that for videocasts you do not need something as expensive as a proper digital video camera. You need to be able to easily upload your finished videocast, and many video upload sites put a limit on file size; even if you rent your own space for hosting the video online, a massive video file will put off or prevent many potential viewers from viewing it. Therefore the expensive digital video camera may be unnecessary or even the wrong tool for the job.

HOW TO RECORD A VIDEOCAST: EDITING SOFTWARE

Most computer cameras and 'proper' digital video cameras come with basic video recording software that will give you all the functionality needed to create a decent video, so you may not need to actively choose editing software.

If you do want to try out editing software, various editing packages are also available for download online, either free of charge or for purchase depending on how much editing power you want. In addition, some online services let you upload your video and edit it online. Here are some examples of video editing software and online services:

- **Microsoft Windows Movie Maker**: This comes free as part of the Windows operating system (XP and Vista). It contains a good selection of editing tools, such as the ability to add titles

- **Avid Free DV** (http://www.avid.com/products/freedv/index.asp): A free editing package for Windows and Apple Mac with a good selection of tools for producing a competent videocast.

- **Jumpcut.com** (http://www.jumpcut.com): A free online service that allows you to upload your videos and edit them online.

- **Moviemasher** (http://www.moviemasher.com): Another free online video editing service.

- **YouTube** (http://www.youtube.com/ytremixer): The popular video website now contains a Remixer feature allowing you to edit videos online.

HOW TO 'PUBLISH' A VIDEOCAST

Podcasts can be hosted on many of the same services that host podcasts, such as Podcast FM. Many services will create an RSS newsfeed for your videocast, allowing the podcast to be obtained through RSS newsreaders. The popular YouTube service can also be used to host videocasts.

MAXIMIZING YOUR AUDIENCE FIGURES

Because videocasts are searchable on search engines such as Google, follow the SEO tips in the Chapter 4 to increase your potential audience.

Social Bookmarking and the 'Online Content Democracy'

In web browsing, bookmarking is the storing of links to web pages that the user finds useful. This allows you to easily go to a web page you use regularly – you simply click on the bookmark. In Internet Explorer, bookmarks are called 'Favorites', and if you want to add a page to your Favorites, click 'Add to Favorites'. All modern web browsers have similar bookmarking technology. As your bookmarks are restricted to one computer, or more accurately one computer account, if someone has a separate login, they will not see your bookmarks and you will not see theirs.

Social bookmarking takes bookmarks and removes the one-user-only barrier. These type of services have been around since the late 1990s, but only became mainstream in 2005/06.

A social bookmarking service acts as a facility for storing your bookmarks. You can of course keep your bookmarks private; even here these services are useful because they mean that your bookmarks can be accessed on whatever computer you happen to be using, without you having to take a file of your bookmarks around with you.

These services come into their own, however, when you start using the sharing facilities. These facilities allow you to make your bookmarks public, or allow access to a specific group of people. Everyone else can do the same, of course, and this is where things become interesting.

Social bookmarking can sometimes be a useful research tool. The most basic type of research is the viewing of bookmarks that other people have stored that fall within a chosen category. This is a great way of picking up new sources of information that you wouldn't previously have known about or regarded as relevant.

Many social bookmarking services do not use a set list of categories. Instead, they use 'tags', which are categories set by the sharer of the bookmark. For example, a bookmark for the Financial Times website might be tagged 'news', 'finance', 'economy', 'UK'.

Social bookmarking has a number of uses and implications that are not immediately obvious:

- They can be used to identify trends.

- You can see what specific people are interested in at any one time. If a leading thinker in your chosen field uses social bookmarks, you can effectively follow what they are interested in at the current time, and draw all sorts of inferences from this.

- Because social bookmarking services indicate who created each bookmark and provide access to that person's other bookmarked resources, users can easily make social connections with other individuals interested in just about any topic.

- Users can also see how many people have used a tag and search for all resources that have been assigned that tag. In this way, the community of users over time will develop a unique structure of keywords to define resources — something that has come to be known as a 'folksonomy'.

- Some services allow you to subscribe to RSS newsfeeds of your chosen categories of interest, allowing you to keep up with those categories simply by adding them to your RSS newsreader (see Chapter 1).

Most social bookmarking services can be accessed free of charge.

Some online services have taken the concept of social bookmarking and used it as the basis for a content site; what content they display is dictated by what their users rate and what they don't, in what has been described by some as an 'online content democracy'. As we will see, what these sites display is not the result of some wonderful popular sentiment, and so maybe 'rankings' site is a more down to earth description than 'democracy'. Below, we look at a traditional social bookmarking service and an online content rankings site.

Del.ic.ious

(http://del.ic.ious)

Del.ic.ious ('delicious') is one of the most popular social bookmarking services, and is owned by Yahoo! The service contains all of the features detailed in above. The service is easy to use, with a smart website and interface. Del.ici. ious was the first well-known site to feature 'tag clouds', a visualization of tags (just yours, a select groups, or all del.ic.ious users). With a tag cloud, the most popular tags are larger than less popular tags, allowing you to visually see what content is most popular. You can see the del.ic.ious all-members tag cloud at http://del.icio.us/tag/.

Del.ic.ious allows users to display their bookmarks on external websites in a number of ways, including latest additions to bookmarks and tag cloud. For bloggers, this means that constantly changing bookmarks can become a feature of their blog (as a replacement to or additional to the standard 'blogroll' list of favourite blogs).

To use del.ic.ious, you have to install software through which you interact with the service. There are a number of different interfaces available, the 'official' ones being that provided on the del.ic.ious website and the Yahoo! Toolbar software. The alternative interfaces are third-party products designed either to take advantage of a particular operating system or computer, or to allow people to use del.ic.ious in a particular way. Once installed, your chosen del. ic.ious interface typically sits within your web browser. The default interface creates buttons within your browser, and you can use these to add websites to your (social) bookmarks, tagging them as part of the process, or to tag a website.

The del.ic.ious website is where you go to view your bookmarks and those of other users. The site has many features:

- You can subscribe to tags, so that the service helps you keep track of the sites that are given that tag by del.ic.ious users.

- If you are friends with another user, or want to keep an eye on what sites they are bookmarking and tagging, you can add them to your 'network'.

- You can view, for a particular tag, the most popular sites given that tag by the entire del.ic.ious community.

- You can view the bookmarks and tags for another user.

- You can subscribe to RSS newsfeeds for tags, so that you can view the latest sites given that tag in your RSS newsreader.

Inevitably, perhaps, the web pages that del.ici.ious is most useful for finding are those on more technical subject matters.

Digg
(http://www.digg.com)

Digg is a user-driven content website. In many ways, it is a social bookmarking service like del.ic.ious. However, it takes the form of a news (or general website page), video and images website. The difference between Digg and a traditional news or entertainment website is that, with Digg, users choose what is displayed. This, claims Digg, gives every bit of web content the chance to be 'the next big thing'.

Digg is in effect a constantly moving chart of the most popular items, as rated by its members. For an item to be displayed on Digg – say, a link to a story on a third party news website – a user must first submit that item to Digg. If other users 'Digg' that site, by clicking on a 'Digg' button next to the item, the item will steadily go up the Digg rankings and could eventually make it to the front page. A popular item will often by 'Digged' a few thousand times. Like del.ic.ious, at the time of writing Digg's users seem to be those interested in technical subjects, so many of the highest rated items are technical in nature, for example, hardware, anti-Microsoft polemic, computer games.

Digg has features designed to encourage discussion around the items it displays. Members can comment on stories; on a popular story this can lead to a large – if not always deeply serious – discussion. These features mean that Digg has a fairly large community of users. Regular Digg users can in time become influential over the rest of the community if they submit and Digg stories that others like. This means that one user can have a big effect over what items become popular.

Digg content can be viewed by its particular category (for example, sports or technology) and by its media type (website, video, etc).

Like many of the other social media discussed in the book, Digg allows users to place its content on their own websites and blogs. This can take the form of a 'widget' for websites/blogs that displays a list of the most popular

Digg items, a top-10 list, or items from a specific source. Digg can also be used within Facebook.

Digg has been at the centre of a number of controversies. Some of these scandals result from a kind of 'mob mentality' that can occur amongst Digg members. For example, in 2006 the editor of an online media company was the subject of accusations that he had stolen Digg code. The story was submitted to Digg, and rapidly rose to the front page because of thousands of Digg members 'Digging' it. Unfortunately, the story was not factually accurate; Digg members had, through the ratings system, publicly attacked someone who they thought had misused Digg. A slightly more innocent example of the mob mentality is the ganging together of Digg members to Digg each others' items, leading those items to get an artificially high placement on the service. In another variation, political or ideological groups have got together to take an item promoting their views to the top of the Digg rankings.

There have also been a number of incidents when companies have paid Digg members to Digg an item, artificially giving it a high placement. Companies or their marketers will approach an influential Digg member and ask them to promote an item in return for payment. When this type of behaviour has been uncovered in the past, Digg has barred the members involved.

There have also been minor controversies as to whether or not Digg itself has edited or even deleted stories submitted to the service, even when those stories have contained no obscene or unlawful content.

All of the above means that the placement of items on Digg should sometimes be taken with a pinch of salt. Just because an item is popular doesn't mean that it is good or an indicator of the latest trend.

How can businesses make use of Digg? First, for finding sources of information you might have otherwise not known about or overlooked, and keeping up with trends, provided that the items on Digg are taken with the previously mentioned pinch of salt. Second, for businesses operating online, Digg is another means of promotion. We certainly don't recommend that you pay Digg users to get your online content to the top of Digg, or use any of the other controversial methods mentioned above; these things tend to be uncovered and this is not going to do your reputation any favours! Instead, if you use Digg as intended, you can over time achieve the presence needed to make its members view the content that you submit. Join up, submit stories, interact in discussions relevant to your subject area. Of course, it is only worth putting in this kind of effort if your online operating is relevant to the Digg demographic.

Forerunners to Social Media

Whilst a lot of the types of social media we will discuss in this chapter you will probably know and use, these types of social media owe a lot to certain internet technologies that have been around for a much longer period. These 'forerunners' allowed internet users to network with each other and distribute their own content, two of the key characteristics of social media.

The discussion of the technologies that follows is not meant to be a history; these technologies are still used by many people, particularly in the technology industry. Those who advise and work with technology businesses are likely to encounter these technologies, and therefore they are just as relevant as any other type of social media.

Electronic Mailing Lists

Not very glamorous, but still in frequent use, electronic mailing lists ('mailing lists') are a means of distributing information to specific groups of people by email. Arguably, the mailing list is the most accessible form of social media; all that most participants in a mailing list need is access to email. The only person that needs more is the organizer of the list, who must have a computer of sufficient power to deal with the day-to-day operation of the mailing list.

A key attraction with mailing lists is that, aside from having to load up an email application (which most people have anyway), there is absolutely no effort involved. No website to find and register with, no software to download, nothing new to learn. Perhaps this is why, despite the advent of more slick forms of online communication and participation, mailing lists continue to be used and new ones continue to be created.

Mailing lists usually take one of two forms. The first is the list that only allows a specific person to contribute to the email, meaning that this is just a mass-email and not something that involves any participation, therefore falling outside our subject area.

The second type allows members of the email group to contribute by emailing a particular address. That email will be handled by the mailing list system in a number of possible ways. The email could simply be distributed to all on the list. Alternatively, it could be collected by the system and distributed in a single email containing all emails sent to the mailing list system that day (or week, or month, or any other period). These emails contain the discussion between the members of the list.

Like other types of social media, mailing lists may be moderated, meaning that someone (a moderator) has the power to say whether an email is distributed to the list at all, or in an edited form.

It's normally quite easy to join a mailing list. You simply have to contact the operator of that list and ask to be placed on the list. You may have to fit certain criteria to be eligible for a particular list (for example, membership of a particular organization), but that's about it.

Mailing lists are the means of communication for many online communities. For example, the Free Software Foundation Europe uses mailing lists as the communication medium for many of it groups, as does Identity Society, a group formed in 2006 to discuss the conceptual and practical issues surrounding digital identity.

How are mailing lists relevant to your business? With the emergence of newer, slicker forms of social media that are easier use, you are unlikely to start a mailing list for your clients, suppliers or sector. However, it is quite possible that clients or suppliers are using mailing lists, so they should not be ruled out.

Usenet Groups

Usenet has its origins back in the 1980s, before the worldwide web evolved. It is an online discussion system, viewed using 'news-reader' software. Usenet remains very popular today, and Microsoft Outlook and some other email applications contain news-readers for this reason.

Usenet groups are hosted on usenet servers. Whether or not you had access to usenet traditionally depended upon on whether your Internet Service

Provider hosted such a server, and, in the workplace, whether your employer allowed access to these servers. In recent years, this issue has to an extent been removed by the emergence of websites that act as usenet readers, such as Google Groups.

Usenet groups take the form of lists of discussion subjects that members of the group can respond to. There are a wide variety of usenet groups on all subjects. Usenet groups are informal and are aimed at and run by individuals rather than businesses.

Like mailing lists, usenet groups are unlikely to be something that businesses will create for external use, but may be of relevance to businesses working in particular industries. Usenet groups may also be of use internally within businesses. For example, many large organizations use internal usenet groups to act as a means of informal communication between people across the organization, or within teams.

Internet Forums

Internet forums are a web-based equivalent to usenet groups and emerged in the mid-to-late 1990s. Forums are discussion groups accessed through a website. There is a wide variety of groups with various different subject matters. Like usenet groups, most internet forums are informal and are aimed at and run by individuals rather than businesses. For businesses, internet forums have little value or potential; the only exception is where there is a group relevant to your target market, or which discusses subjects relevant to your professional interests.

Social Media Aggregators

CHAPTER 14

The rapid rise in popularity of social media has been accompanied by the proliferation of social media websites. If you regularly use more than a couple of social media services, you may find yourself logging into each service a few times a day. This soon adds up to a lot of time-consuming clicking through websites.

As we saw in the Chapter 1, RSS newsfeed readers save you time when reading blogs by putting all the blog content in one place. Similar solutions have been developed for other types of social media. These solutions are generically called social media aggregators. To date, social media aggregators have tended to work for social and professional networking sites, and some content distribution sites, but not for other types of social media such as wikis and virtual worlds. An expansion of compatibility into these other types of social media is likely to occur in the future, and maybe by the time this book is published.

Two social media aggregators are described below.

Spokeo
(http://www.spokeo.com)

An easy-to-use tool, Spokeo lets you start adding links to your friends content on social media sites straight away. Spokeo works with:

- networking sites such as MySpace;

- content distribution sites such as YouTube;

- social bookmarking sites such as Digg;

- blogging services like Blogger.

At the time of writing, Spokeo did not work with popular networking sites such as LinkedIn and Facebook, making Profilactic a more powerful option.

Profilactic

(http://www.profilactic.com)

Profilactic claims to be able to 'pull in just about everything you and your friends create online'. Able to take content from over 60 different social media services – more than this book could possibly cover – verifies this claim, at least to an extent. Profilactic works with:

- networking sites such as LinkedIn and Facebook;
- content distribution sites such as Flickr and Vox;
- social bookmarking sites such as Digg;
- online RSS newsfeed aggregators such as Google Reader.

As with other social media aggregators, Profilactic does not work for other types of social media such as virtual worlds and wikis.

Profilactic is easy to use, although its interface is more messy and complicated than Spokeo's.

PART 3

Using Social Media Internally

Social Tools Inside the Enterprise

In recent years, we have witnessed a rapid growth in the use of social tools, such as wikis, blogs, social bookmarking and social networking inside businesses as an alternative to existing heavy-duty enterprise software. These tools are often very attractive to users because of their simplicity, ease of use and adaptability. They are orders of magnitude simpler than 1990s-era enterprise systems, partly because they have learned the lessons about what works on the consumer internet.

The tools themselves are very good, but what makes them really stand out from previous generations of collaboration and community tools is the fact that they target individual benefits as a route to shared value, rather than asking people to share for collective benefit. This approach of networked individualism has proven far more successful in generating high levels of participation and shared value creation than before. Powerful network effects are generated by focusing on incentivizing and supporting individual action and then aggregating the results of these individual actions upwards for all to share. Wikipedia is one of the most well-known examples of this phenomenon. A wiki for one is just a useful note-taking tool, but a wiki for thousands of people can become a comprehensive, community-maintained encyclopaedia.

This change in tools and behaviours reflects a progressive shift from the physical economy towards a knowledge economy. While value creation shifts from muscle sweat to brain juice, traditionally detailed and task-oriented processes need to be enriched because they are no longer appropriate for knowledge-based production. Previous generations of enterprise systems are largely based on the factory model of knowledge sharing – mass collection and processing, centralized repositories and a one-size-fits-all mentality. Future generations will be closer to the model of a hive – joining together lots of individual actions and signals to create new forms of collective intelligence. Whereas knowledge sharing used to focus on transporting documents and packaged objects as explicit representations of knowledge, we are now more interested in the processes that underpin informal knowledge sharing within social networks.

Within knowledge-intensive companies, such as law firms and the professional services sector, this new approach is finding fertile ground. In particular, there is growing interest in the creation of competitive advantage through the improvement of knowledge capture and deployment to advise on complex issues affecting their clients. Enterprise social software has tremendous potential within legal and professional service contexts where dealing with complexity is a key source of value. When appropriately implemented, managed and used within a supportive organizational culture and structure, these tools can assist people to deal better with ambiguity and exercise high levels of judgement, through effectively harnessing the collective intelligence and deep experience within the organization. In practice, complex interactions represent part of the spectrum of work undertaken within professional service contexts, and are ordinarily combined with – and fed by – more commoditized information processing. Social tools have a role to play here as well, making it easier to cope with large information flows by using the power of social networks to filter out the useful or actionable insight.

The potential application of social tools goes beyond knowledge sharing and current awareness, however, and extends to client relationship management, recruitment, employee retention and marketing. In general, the benefits that organizations are seeking from the adoption of such tools include:

- better communication and collaboration amongst staff at all levels across practices and sectors;

- better client and market knowledge capturing current knowledge that is relevant to current contexts and situations;

- more shared discussion of client and firm matters;

- better decision making;

- increased self-service and self-reliance based on a wider and constantly updated pool of information;

- timely delivery and more efficient and streamlined processes with regard to knowledge/information exchange;

- capture of knowledge as part of the work process (rather than a separate activity) transforming the tacit into the tangible;

- better recruitment, retention and morale;

- better and more learning opportunities for professionals such as lawyers or consultants, particularly junior and pre-qualified professionals, and trainees.

Social tools bring something of a new 'reality' to information systems. Previous solutions were designed in a simple and straightforward way: one problem, one solution. The world of IT was populated with a vast number of specific solutions solving specific, limited, well-defined issues, but the majority of the time, people find that their specific needs do not fit neatly into one of these problem–solution combinations. Social tools work differently, in the sense that you can address many organizational needs with one tool or a combination of tools. For instance, a blogging platform can prove useful for internal communications, external communication, team and project management as well as expert-based knowledge management.

Whilst many organizations have now taken their first steps with pilot projects and experiments looking at individual tools such as a blog or a wiki, the next stage of evolution will be about how these tools are combined to create an enterprise social software platform that can support a range of different use cases for different groups. Within the present author's company, Headshift, we use the concept of a social 'stack' to understand how we can combine different tools and their corresponding interaction modes to support different workplace needs (see Figure 15.1).

We think of this as creating a knowledge pyramid that filters raw information into actionable knowledge and insight. At the base sits a wide, open system of RSS/Atom newsfeeds generated from internal and external sources. By providing people with simple tools to bookmark or grab items from within this river of news, we allow them to not only organize their own information, but also to generate social signals about relevance. This filtered sub-set of information can then be used to inform conversations and discussions on blogs or within teams, whose insight and analysis based on these sources also gets pushed back out into the 'flow'. When people identify actionable knowledge and want to do something about it, they can take it into wiki-based collaboration groups where they are able to co-produce knowledge outputs that can be used, shared or exported into formal repositories. At the top of the pyramid, tying all this activity together, might be a personal portal or personal start page along the lines of Netvibes or iGoogle, which makes it easy for an individual to manage their participation in multiple groups, track their newsfeeds and perhaps mediate access to other systems as well.

Figure 15.1   Introduction to the 'social stack'

Background image source: http://www.flickr.com/photos/86624586@N00/10190970/

To realize the benefits of social tools also requires a shift in behaviour and perception regarding the management of knowledge and current awareness. Principally, it requires participation from professionals at all levels to take advantage of network effects derived from aggregating user behaviour and inputs at scale. In other words, the value these tools offer depends on regular contributions, networked thinking and good levels of participation. Key to this is a gradual move towards self-service and making knowledge capture part of everybody's day-to-day roles, rather than being attributable to individual support people. Larger firms have the potential to recreate the dynamics of online public social networks and knowledge sharing inside the firm because of their scale. Smaller firms and sole consultants/practitioners can also enjoy similar benefits by operating in a similar way within their market as a whole.

We have tended to build roles on the same factory-based view of knowledge sharing as was present in the first generation of enterprise knowledge management systems, which tended to emphasize standalone individual applications with centralized content management, storage and classification rather than interpersonal interaction and collaboration. They were built upon a specific, ontological conception of knowledge: knowledge = data. Typically, such systems were over-engineered and suffered from poor usability and adaptability. Enterprise content management systems reduced workflow to permission and conversation to versioning, and people have been forced to resort to email for far too much of their knowledge-sharing activity as a result. Storing content in firm-wide systems is seen as a chore rather than a core way of working. But even where these systems are well embedded within firms, and people are using them in their daily work, they are focused more on supporting individual search and find behaviours than knowledge sharing and networking, and as a result, they fail to take advantage of the potential scale of the communities of practice and networks that exist within large knowledge-intensive firms.

In the next two chapters, we will examine how social media provide a technological means for knowledge sharing and interaction within organizations, and look at some examples of social media put into action.

Elements of 'Enterprise 2.0'

CHAPTER

16

The business application of Web 2.0 ideas is sometimes referred to as 'Enterprise 2.0'[1], derived from the title of an *MIT Sloan Management Review* article by Professor Andrew McAfee in the Spring 2006 edition. In the article, McAfee surveys some of the available case study and survey data about the use of Web 2.0 tools inside large organizations, and talks about the potential for 'emergent collaboration' to make both the practice and outputs of 'knowledge work' more visible within companies.[2]

Successful Enterprise 2.0 projects often combine various tools, data services and applications, joined together by shared protocols and 'signals' such as RSS and Atom generated from enterprise- or market-based networks (which notify users when information of interest to them has been published/updated). This means they are generally cheaper, more adaptable and lower risk than existing enterprise systems, as they do not depend upon a single overarching platform, that is, it is possible to cherry pick elements of the system, integrating or replacing them with other tools without having to dispose of the whole system.

A typical Enterprise 2.0 platform for knowledge-intensive firms is underpinned by a combination of infrastructure, software tools, services and data, namely:

- aggregation and subscription

- blogging

- social bookmarking and collaborative filtering

- social tagging

---

1   D. Hinchliffe (2006) 'Web 2.0 definition updated and Enterprise 2.0 emerges', http://blogs. zdnet.com/Hinchcliffe/?p=71.

2   A. McAffee (2006) 'Enterprise 2.0: The Dawn of Emergent Collaboration' (Reprint 47306), *MIT Sloan Management* Review, Vol. 47, No. 3, pp. 21–28.

- wiki-based group collaboration

- social networking

- personalized pages.

Such tools, on their own or together as part of a social stack, should ideally complement and integrate with rather than replace existing systems, although they can normally be expected to result in reduced dependence upon email and content management systems, which is often seen as a success measure for many firms who are aware that over-reliance on email is a major productivity drain.

Aggregation and Subscription

This is the key underlying element of infrastructure that has driven the adoption of social tools, and it provides the bedrock of subscription and aggregation that allows people in knowledge-based organizations to share information quickly and easily. This is part of what Professor McAfee refers to as the 'signals' piece of Enterprise 2.0.

Instead of thinking about content management based on individual items, aggregation systems focus on managing feeds (flows) that consist of information from a person, team or organization, or perhaps a saved search, news alert or new subject area. One of the basic principles of Web 2.0 is that every content item should have a link that does not change (a permalink). Similarly, every area of content generation (for example, a blog, wiki or hot topics page) should have a feed that users can subscribe to without constantly checking back to see what is new or what has changed. In a law firm, for example, this means that lawyers could subscribe to an internal legal blog that discusses new government legislation instead of trying to find competent lawyers internally by any other means.

As a transport mechanism, news feeds (RSS, Atom, and so on) offer the best hope of moving away from email as the default vehicle for knowledge sharing within professional services companies, as they give individuals greater control over their information inputs and enable a larger volume of information to be handled without the archiving and filing overheads of an email client.

Blogging

Blogs are widely deployed throughout many organizations to improve the flow and quality of information and both internal and external awareness of what is going on. Corporate blogs are currently used for a variety of purposes, including internal communication and knowledge sharing, marketing, customer relations and external PR. Some professional services firms use internal newsletter blogs, for example, instead of publishing email or printed newsletters. This has the advantages of speed, cost and interactivity, as colleagues can comment directly on the articles posted.

In addition to the immediate benefits derived from increasing the volume and flow of informal knowledge and information sharing, corporate blogs are also extremely useful as network building tools because they are participatory communication tools that can stimulate discussion within networks, teams, firms and markets. Corporate blogs can be used in individual and group modes; they can be highly functional or free-form and discursive. In either case, the usefulness of blogs increases with network size and level of connectedness (see Figure 16.1).

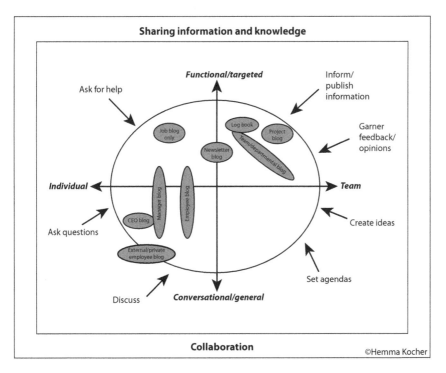

Figure 16.1   Sharing information and knowledge

Some examples of successful corporate and legal/professional services blogs include:

- Legal firm Allen & Overy employs group blogs based on interest groups, teams and communities of practice.

- Staff at Dresdner Kleinwort Wasserstein and at the BBC in London maintain internal corporate blogs.[3] They use these blogs to share current awareness and work on projects together. The research department at the Deutsche Bank in Frankfurt uses a departmental blog that is used as a log book. Staff update each other giving brief information on their daily business.[4]

- Siemens, McDonalds, General Motors and SAP have CEO and senior management blogs – see, for example, http://csr.blogs.mcdonalds. com/ or http://boeingblogs.com/randy/

Social Bookmarking and Collaborative Filtering

Social bookmarking is a phenomenally simple way of sharing links to useful sites, pages or documents. Instead of saving links in a web browser, which are hard to manage beyond a few dozen links, users click a button in their browser to save a link plus optional information such as keywords (tags) and a description to a central bookmarking service. These are then organized by the tags a user has applied, and can be shared by others to whom the user gives access.

When enough people use the service, such as on the internet (http://www. connotea.org, http://del.icio.us and http://ma.gnolia.com) or within a large law firm, interesting network effects begin to emerge, such as the ability to subscribe to a specific tag to receive all bookmarks people have categorized under that term, or a specific person's bookmarks if they have domain expertise. Also, by aggregating the links people bookmark, useful information becomes available about what people think is important (rather than just links they follow), and the terms people use to categorize things they have found.

---

3   Deutsche Bank (2005) 'The new magic formula for corporate communication', Frankfurt, Deutsch Bank Research, http://www.dbresearch.com/PROD/DBR_Internet_ En-PROD/PROD0000000000190745.pdf.

4   H. Kocher, H (2006) 'The Role of Corporate Internal Blogs for Internal Communication', MA thesis, Bournemouth University, UK.

This approach to distributing the gathering of useful links and news items across the organization has tremendous potential to improve the flow of information and awareness of what's going on within a law firm. If we know who is bookmarking which links, and what keywords they apply to them, we can build up a very accurate picture of what the real 'hot topics' are inside the enterprise, based on people's day-to-day-activity.

This is analogous to the collaborative filtering that Amazon.com pioneered in the 1990s ('people who read X also read Y') and is emerging as a major potential source of collective intelligence within large organizations. In knowledge-based firms, social newsreading, where people contribute to current awareness through their reading, linking and bookmarking, is one of the most important developments in Enterprise 2.0.

Below are some examples of social bookmarking in action:

- Employees at Allen & Overy share their group and individual bookmarks following what colleagues read and find important.

- IBM uses its own application 'dogear' to bookmark and tag useful links within the company and external web links. Thousands of users contribute to this store of useful material, and the resulting tag cloud representations have become a kind of corporate radar, showing what different parts of the business are focusing on at any given time (http://domino.watson.ibm.com/cambridge/research.nsf/242252765710c19485256979004d289c/1c181ee5fbcf59fb852570fc0052ad75).

- The Mitre Corporation has published a useful study about its use of social bookmarking and its potential role in the modern enterprise (http://www.mitre.org/work/tech_papers/tech_papers_06/06_0352/06_0352.pdf).

Social Tagging

Social tagging is the application of free-text tags (keywords) to content items for ease of retrieval later on, but within a social context that enables others to see and share the tags applied by others.

The application of meaningful metadata to stored content has been a constant challenge for companies who have traditionally attempted to apply one top-down taxonomy across the firm and require individuals to use this corporate taxonomy to navigate and classify content. Many firms have discovered that this results in an unwieldy and impractical classification system that tries to define all human knowledge, and as a result is full of contradictions and compromise between what works and what makes sense.

Social tagging, by contrast, tackles the issue from the opposite angle. It allows individuals to quickly and simply apply tags that they find useful, and that will help them organize their own content in a way that suits them. But by aggregating upwards the tags being used by a large population, with some measure of popularity and recency, the emergent metadata that results is often a far more accurate reflection of the themes and issues people are dealing with across the law firm. Social tagging need not be entirely without structure, since faceted tag clouds can be applied (for example, project tags, client tags, sector tags) to provide multiple views on the same content.

On the public internet, the principal reason tagging has taken off so quickly and become so widespread is ease of use. Formal taxonomies impose a high cost of classification on individuals working with content, but the benefits of doing so are not immediately apparent. By contrast, social tagging imposes a much lower cost, whilst giving users the immediate benefit of organizing content in a way that makes it easy to find again, and yet still generates collective benefits of shared classification and negotiated meaning.

There are many examples of innovative uses of social tagging for knowledge sharing in (legal and professional services) companies:

- Lucent uses social tagging for navigation of library content (http://urlgreyhot.com/personal/node/2463).

- US Interactive agency 'Avenue A'/Razorfish uses the public social bookmarking service del.icio.us to allow anybody to suggest links for its intranet (http://www.alexbarnett.net/blog/archive/2006/11/19/Tagging-behind-the-firewall-_2D00_-a-case-study.aspx).

Wiki-based Group Collaboration

So far, we have looked at tools and modes of interaction that help knowledge/information flow into the system and be filtered, ranked and structured. Alongside this, people need similarly easy and accessible ways to work together with this information to turn it into actionable insight. Wikis are ideally suited for this role, and are now widely used for document co-writing, the creation of knowledge repositories and glossaries, idea generation/brainstorming, and project-based collaboration.

Given wikis' high level of flexibility and configurability, the degree of structure and openness can be determined by, or emerge from, the particular needs of the project, community or task. Not all wikis are flat and open. Highly granular permissions in enterprise wiki platforms can provide control over access and edit rights, enabling different groups to interact with specific areas in different ways. In the majority of cases, however, greater network effects can be realized and collective intelligence gathered from open wikis, where all users (within the firewall) are able to contribute, edit and maintain content. The tagging, linking and categorizing behaviours seen in other social tools are also present in a good wiki platform to support the creation of useful, structured, searchable, navigable wiki spaces. As new content is created, the wiki pages themselves add to the flow of knowledge/information into the system through the use of RSS feeds.

Common use cases for wikis include the creation of knowledge bases, documentation, case studies, project management information and specific areas of intellectual property creation. Contributions to, and maintenance of, wiki content is, of course, particularly dependent on participative behaviours and people taking responsibility for updating information, adding links and sharing their ideas/experiences/analysis. Participation can be encouraged through demonstrating practical benefits, such as the ease of writing and versioning a document using a wiki compared to email and a word processing tool, or the ease with which the wiki can aid in the capture of tacit knowledge (which could otherwise be lost in casual/social problem solving encounters). But encouraging a culture of wiki usage – 'if it's broken, fix it!' – is very important to successful usage.

Business Social Networking

Thanks to the success of MySpace, Facebook and other personal online social networks, similar systems are being considered inside the firewall to revive tired corporate directories, which are not particularly effective as expertise locators. There are already thousands of people profiles on business social networking sites such as LinkedIn (http://www.linkedin.com) and Xing (https://www.xing.com), which suggests this approach is not entirely new. These services are excellent at building connections outside the company and can prove very useful for client acquisitions.

But social networking also delivers value within organizations by complementing the traditional representation through organization charts that, in fact, only represent formal authority. Social networks help mapping the informal, often hidden coordination that helps people deliver. This is particularly true when linking personal profiles to the links, blog posts and tags associated with an individual. They can also prove very useful during reorganizations or mergers.

Personalized Pages

Personalized pages are an increasingly popular form of organizer on the internet, and sites like Netvibes and iGoogle are very popular ways of doing this. They can create coherence without the rigidity of content management systems or hard-to-use enterprise portal systems. Personal start pages help people navigate and make sense of their 'digital life' both inside and outside the corporate firewall, and their popularity seems to be directly related to their ease of use.

Social Media Case Studies and Conclusions

There are many examples of the use of enterprise social tools available on the internet to review, through sites such as Cases2 (http://www.cases2.com) and the 'Case Studies' section of the Headshift website (http://www.headshift.com/projects). Two case studies concerning the use of social tools inside a top tier global law firm and a leading international audit firm are summarized below.

SOCIAL GROUPWARE FOR LAWYERS[1]

Social media consultancy firm Headshift's work with Allen & Overy focused on three core needs:

1. internal work communities with ongoing communication and collaboration;

2. project teams working on new areas of law with knowledge creation/capture and existing information sharing;

3. facilitation of general internal communications.

Once we had performed an initial needs assessment, we engaged discrete groups and leaders who were enthusiastic about using social tools and developing more collaborative behaviour. These people would become very important in the later encouragement of participation and transfer of best practices to other groups in the firm. Also, focusing on discrete business needs, and a number of very specific scenarios and use cases, helped simplify the process of working with new tools and make the best use of available time by concentrating on real problems and issues that needed to be solved.

---

1   R. Ward (2006) 'Wiki's Law: Case Study – Allen & Overy', *Inside Knowledge* 9(10).

We then built a prototype group collaboration system consisting of a wiki, group blog, shared bookmarking, social tagging tool and a news aggregator, all integrated within a simple common interface developed by working with group members in workshops.

Each site (or group space) is open only to 'members' but also has a public blog for members to present their work to the rest of the firm and allow outsiders to comment and provide feedback on it. The home page of each site contains an overview of latest discussions (in the form of group blog posts), popular themes within discussions, recent wiki page changes and bookmarks.

Many of the workflows we targeted with the early pilot groups are about improving workflows that previously were supported only by email and document exchange (using enterprise content management systems), as Figure 17.1 and Figure 17.2 illustrate.

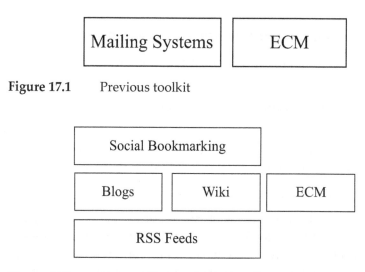

Figure 17.1   Previous toolkit

Figure 17.2   Current 'Enterprise 2.0' toolkit

When information is posted on the blogs, or created/updated in the wiki, the author of the information can decide whether to notify group members with an immediate email alert or send an aggregated daily alert of all changes. Daily alerts also contain a summary of blog/wiki page changes. When logged in, group members can see the most recent group blog posts and navigate to the full content via a link. Alternatively, members can view content using:

- **Categories**: Pre-defined site-specific groupings that constitute a form of filing that helps people to navigate through the content on the site.

- **Tags**: A more homogenous grouping system that provides topical search capability allowing people to find collections of posts tagged with that name (within the group area or in other areas where 'restricted' public viewing may apply). Existing tags can be selected and applied to the post or new tags created as appropriate.

- **Date archive**: That is, viewing the months in which posts were created.

- **Search functionality**: Unlike categories (which form a cascading list), tags appear in an alphabetical cloud. Tags are a particularly useful feature of the site, as they provide an effective visual representation of popular topics: the more a tag is used in relation to posts, the bigger it appears in the cluster of tags (or 'tagcloud'). People can also share their group and personal bookmarks, enabling others to tap into valuable web sources and stay abreast of current topics that others are reading/find important, without having to trawl through complete journals or sources.

Over time, the group blogs/discussions have replaced various email interest groups and ad-hoc emails sent out with news of upcoming events, new joiners and other general firm information, decreasing the time needed to coordinate activities or raise awareness of current issues. Since the project first started in 2005, the number of posts as well as the readership has increased. Moreover, self-help and shared ownership of content has resulted in less administration and more pro-active communication throughout the firm. Currently, over 30 per cent of the firm's staff are members of one or more groups, and the number of groups has expanded from the original three pilot groups to around 40, most of which are internal, but some of which exist across the firewall to facilitate collaboration with key clients.

ENRICHING TRAINING AND FACILITATING EMPLOYEE RETENTION: A LEADING INTERNATIONAL AUDIT FIRM

As part of its forward strategy, the firm recognized that employees are its most significant asset and put a strong emphasis on both employee training and retention, particularly the juniors.

Our work consisted of implementing a collaborative solution based on in-depth interaction with future users. A great proportion of the audience already use social media in their personal life and had experienced enriched university directories based on social network applications. The findings of the consulting phase highlighted a strong will for using social and collaborative tools. However, because users recognized this was about 'work', they were keen to have something that felt meaningful, focusing on work-related functionality.

As a result, a wiki-based solution was developed that:

- Centralizes all training information in one on-line location. The firm gains consistency in training documentation, which impacts the quality of training, cuts the cost of materials (virtually no paper) and decreases time in finding and accessing information.

- Diffuses information such as events and news around training with an alumni approach, which builds momentum and demand for communication and training.

- Allows peer-to-peer support as a way of bringing the social touch to training. Employees can benefit from each other's knowledge in context, which is closer to the experience of day-to-day office work.

Conclusion

The new wave of enterprise social tools are transforming the way we think about IT within companies. IT projects no longer need to be measured in millions of pounds and years of elapsed time – social tools are built around rapid iteration and learning from user behaviour and feedback. Best-of-breed social tools typically provide a lightweight dynamic platform emphasizing interpersonal interaction, collaboration and the benefits of network effects as the basis for internal applications.

Enterprise social computing promotes participation from people at all organizational levels, from collaborative document writing to social bookmarking and content tagging, making knowledge capture part of the everyday work process. It helps bridge a key gap between the current (over)use of emails and enterprise content management systems for collaborative purposes, whilst offering a smoother workflow from idea generation to structured outputs. Newsfeeds are creating greater flow within networks, and tools such as social bookmarking and tagging are making it very easy for people to find what they need and create valuable social signals about relevance in the process. On top of these, blogs are being used for discussion and knowledge sharing, and wikis are providing a very simple and adaptable collaboration platform that helps people organize and re-factor knowledge within the enterprise. The key lesson in our experience is that no one tool or system should be used to the exclusion of all others. The best results we have seen derive from using a blend of social tools in a situated context.

The greater the level of participation in the use of these tools and contribution to collaborative activities, the greater the result in terms of network effects and collective intelligence benefits. In the future, as organizations develop capabilities in the use of enterprise social computing internally, the potential for extending usage externally, to client relationship management, recruitment and marketing presents interesting opportunities and challenges, not least of which will be the eventual involvement of clients within the collective intelligence creation process, in order to develop crucial collaborative exchanges creating differentiation and competitive advantage later adopters will struggle to emulate.

10 Tips for Social Software Deployment in the Enterprise

Through our work with organizations in a number of sectors, including in the legal and professional services sector, we have gained considerable experience in refining and/or enhancing business processes through carefully managed implementation of social software tools. The following 10 tips summarize key activities that should be considered when starting any social software project:

1.   Identify a key need (or needs) to be addressed.

2.   Start small and work with just a few groups, isolating how current behaviours/routines and use of existing systems impact on the need(s).

3.   Focus on the groups who are enthusiastic and committed to adoption of new tools and ways of working (so that they spread the word).

4.   Involve those groups in the establishment of clear goals/business objectives for the implementation.

5.   Identify the main site owner and other champions early in the process to develop people within the groups who will create momentum and encourage organic growth/adoption.

6.   Establish the requirements for the implementation and how they relate to the business goals and the change processes to be undertaken, including business and cultural implications.

7.   Select software to meet the goals/business objects, rather than trying to implement new tools for their own sake.

8.   Ensure the tools are easy to use and that people are clear as to how their use relates to the goals/business objectives (so that you save time and money on training) .

9.   Manage the expectations of the site owner(s) in terms of initial site support.

10.   Seek feedback continuously to learn how people can best be supported in their work and the tools tailored (progressively enriched) accordingly.

PART 4

Social Media and The Law

The Law of Social Media[1]

CHAPTER

18

This chapter provides an overview of some of the key legal issues associated with blogging and using social media under the laws of England and Wales. It aims to equip users of the social web with a basic level of knowledge of the relevant laws in the UK, including both the risks and users' rights. It also addresses some of the ways that the law has adapted to face the new challenges of the social web and how service providers have been affected. The speed with which the web has developed in recent years has resulted in many issues remaining untested by the courts, so by necessity some of our analysis is speculative, based on disputes that have been settled before reaching the courts, or on cases from other jurisdictions where different laws may apply.

This chapter is structured as follows, with sections addressing a number of the key areas of the law that apply to the social web:

- Introduction: social media and the law

- Copyright

- Brand protection – trade marks, passing off and domain names

- Defamation

- Privacy and data protection

- Employment and blogging

- E-commerce and the 'hosting' exemption

- User contracts and terms of use

- Jurisdiction

- Summing up – other issues and the future.

---

1   This chapter is not intended to constitute advice in relation to any particular legal issue. If readers require advice on any of the issues raised, they should seek legal advice from a qualified solicitor.

Introduction: Social Media and the Law

Hailed for their democratizing influence and enthusiastically embraced by millions of people across the world, social media typify the new shape of the internet. Dubbed 'Web 2.0', they are characterized by collaboration, users generating their own content and websites that succeed by 'harnessing collective intelligence'.[2] It is a 'social web' that is built and ordered by its users.

THE ROLE OF LAW IN ORDERING THE SOCIAL WEB

The tools of the social web have allowed people to communicate through innovative channels, but they have also given rise to their own social structures, including the playful communities of Facebook 'groups', the huge amorphous 'blogosphere', and the virtual worlds of Second Life and World of Warcraft.

As facilitators of social interaction, it is no surprise that social media have played host to a wide range of social and legal issues, many of which are familiar from the 'real' world. There are disputes, transactions, collaborations and assertions of rights. But of course the inhabitants of the social web are still governed by the laws of the real world, so we have seen social media act as forums for exploring and testing the limits of our existing laws, many of which were created long before even the internet was conceived.

In addition, some of the new risks raised by the developing technologies of the social web are also 'public' issues that result in government intervention through statute, such as the new offence of 'grooming' under the Sexual Offences Act 2003,[3] addressing concerns about the use of chat rooms by paedophiles.

The participants in the social web have also demanded the creation of their own bespoke rules to meet the new requirements of the communities of the social web. Some of these are discrete 'private' rules established by the new communities themselves. So users of Second Life are required to abide by comprehensive Terms of Service and Community Standards (see http://secondlife.com/app/help/rules/cs.php), addressing prohibited behaviour in the Second Life world, and breach may result in 'Suspension' or 'Banishment'. Wikipedia has rules for handling disputes between contributing 'Wikipedians' (http://en.wikipedia.org/wiki/Wikipedia:Resolving_disputes), and even an arbitration panel for unresolved disputes (http://en.wikipedia.org/wiki/Wikipedia:Arbitration_committee).

---

2   O'Reilly Media, Inc. (2008) 'What is Web 2.0?', http://www.oreillynet.com/pub/a/oreilly/tim/news/2005/09/30/what-is-web-20.html?page=2.

3   Sexual Offences Act 2003, Section 15.

It is no surprise that these communities, characterized by user participation, should also see users involved in their own legislative processes and the enforcement of the rules. For instance, Wikipedians are involved in debating and developing the rules for contributors (http://en.wikipedia.org/wiki/Wikipedia: Policies_and_guidelines) and enforcing them on other users by deleting or editing inappropriate content. Even the guilds of World of Warcraft write their own rules of conduct. The Phoenix Legion's Guild Charter states: 'We do not tolerate dude speak' (http://phoenixlegion.co.uk/guild-charter/). Members who do not comply may find that they are dismissed from the Legion – the Charter makes it clear that the officers' decision is final.

THE RISKS OF THE SOCIAL WEB

For the average person, the laws applicable to social media have presented their own challenge. Professional journalists may be well used to working within (or on the edge of) the laws that apply to writing and publishing, but now amateur bloggers are required to understand the principles of defamation, intellectual property infringement and privacy. The opportunities of the social web go hand in hand with the risks. Everything a blogger writes forms part of a permanent, searchable repository that is available everywhere all the time. The ease with which people can contribute to the social web belies the complexity of some of the accompanying legal issues.

Generally, though, just as the new societies of the web have tended to shape themselves into familiar hierarchies (in Second Life, the economy of the Linden Dollar behaves rather similarly to 'real world' economies – http://randolfe. typepad.com/randolfe/2007/01/secondlife_revo.html), there have been few surprises in the application of existing laws to social media. There is no new law of blogging; more frequently, existing legal principles are reaffirmed by their application to interactions taking place through social media.

Copyright

Copyright owners have the right to prevent others from copying their works. The law on copyright protects the form of those works (for example, the actual words or music – see below) rather than the ideas expressed in those works. So when the authors and publishers of *The Da Vinci Code* were sued by the authors of an earlier book, *The Holy Blood and The Holy Grail*, the Court of Appeal held[4] that *The Da Vinci Code* did not infringe copyright because, among other

---

4   *Baigent and Leigh v The Random House Group Limited* (2007) EWCA Civ 247.

things, the material allegedly copied consisted of ideas rather than the actual expression (text) of the earlier book.

Unlike some other intellectual property rights such as patents, copyright does not give owners a monopoly right over their works, so in theory two authors could create identical works and each separately own copyright in the works they create provided they work wholly independently and do not 'copy' each others' work.

COPYRIGHT – THE LAW

What is copyright and who owns it?

Copyright arises automatically in the UK and so there is no need to register a work to benefit from copyright protection. This can be contrasted with the USA, where additional rights may be obtained through registration. However, a work must fall within a specific list of categories in order to be protected, of which the ones most relevant to users of the social web are the following:

- original 'literary' works – which could include the text of blogs and wikis, the lyrics of songs shared through YouTube and the html code underlying a website;

- dramatic, musical and artistic works – for example in the music of a song shared through YouTube, or in a drawing displayed on a social networking site homepage; and

- sound recordings, films and broadcasts – including the recording of a film or song.

If the work is a literary, dramatic or musical work, it will not be protected by copyright until it is recorded (in writing or otherwise). In addition, works will only be protected under UK copyright if at the time of publishing the material the author was a British citizen, or was domiciled or resident in the UK, or the work was first published in the UK. The duration of copyright varies depending on the category of work. For example, copyright in literary works such as blog posts lasts for the life of the author plus 70 years from the end of the calendar year in which the author dies. Copyright in sound recordings lasts for 50 years after the year in which the recording was made or first released (though the record industry has been lobbying for an extension).

Generally, the author of a work will own the copyright in that work. However, where a work is made by an employee in the course of their employment, the employer will be the owner of the copyright, subject to any contrary agreement.

Regardless of who owns the copyright, authors of some categories of works (including literary works such as blogs and musical works such as songs) also have certain moral rights. Moral rights include the right to be identified as the author or director of the copyright work, the right to object to derogatory treatment of a copyright work and the right not to have a copyright work falsely attributed. An employee will only have limited moral rights where the copyright in a work is owned by their employer.

How can copyright be infringed?

The copyright owner has the exclusive right to copy a work (for example, by reproducing the text of a blog post), issue copies to the public (for example, by placing a song or movie on a file-sharing site), perform, show or play it in public, communicate the work to the public (which might include streaming over the internet) or make an adaptation of a copyright work. A third party who, without consent, does any of these acts will commit primary copyright infringement. In addition, a person who deals with an article that they know or have reason to believe is an infringing copy will commit secondary infringement.

To establish copyright infringement, claimants must show that a substantial amount of the work in question has been copied, and this is judged by reference to what has been copied rather than how much. If a whole article is copied then clearly this will constitute copyright infringement; however, a small but critical part of a work may also be 'substantial' (such as a refrain from a song).

There is no requirement for an intention to infringe and therefore a writer can infringe copyright in a work without knowing that their actions are an infringement. It is even possible to infringe the copyright in a work without having seen the work, for example if the writer has been given information from the original or seen a recreation of the original.

Copyright owners may be entitled to recover any profits made by infringing parties from copying their works, or an injunction to prevent further infringement.

What are the defences?

There are only a limited number of defences to copyright infringement, based on the concept of 'fair dealing'. These include fair dealing for the purposes of criticism or review, which might apply to bloggers reviewing new movies and music, and fair dealing for the purpose of news reporting, which might apply in the context of blogging journalists. It is not yet clear how far the fair dealing for news reporting defence will be stretched now that every blogger might claim to be an amateur journalist. To qualify for one of the fair dealing defences an author's work must also contain a sufficient acknowledgement (that is, generally the author copying the relevant section must acknowledge the author by name).

There is no statutory guidance about when dealing is 'fair', but the courts have considered factors such as whether the alleged infringing use competes commercially with the copyright owner's exploitation of their work, whether the copyright work has already been published or made available to the public (if not, it will be harder to establish that the dealing is fair) and the amount and importance of the part of the work copied (was it necessary to copy the amount copied?).

COPYRIGHT AND SOCIAL MEDIA

It is easy to see how the growth of the internet and the increasing popularity of blogging has resulted in an increase in copyright infringement. The multimedia world of the social web is littered with copyright materials, which may or may not be reproduced with the consent of the rights owners. Photographs posted to Facebook and Flickr, films and music posted to YouTube and materials posted on a blog may all be the subject of copyright protection but come from a variety of sources. For example, a blogger might copy text from an article or a photograph belonging to another without permission for their own blog post. Users infringing the rights of copyright owners risk being sued for infringement. For instance, the British Phonographic Industry, which represents the record companies and other major stakeholders in the UK music industry, started (successfully) taking legal action against members of file-sharing communities for copyright infringement in 2005.[5]

Service providers also run the risk of being exposed to claims of copyright infringement. Most famously, Napster was found liable in the USA for contributing to the infringement of copyright by its users, who were sharing music files over a peer-to-peer network.[6] More recently, though again in the USA, the musician Prince has reportedly required YouTube to remove infringing

---

5   'Peter' (2005) 'BPI sues file sharers', Naked Law, http://nakedlaw.typepad.com/naked_law/2005/08/the_bpi_has_iss.html.
6   *A&M Records, Inc v Napster, Inc* 239 F.3d 1004 (9th circuit 2001).

copies of his music, and has threatened to sue YouTube (currently owned by Google) for contributory infringement.[7]

The bloggers' guide: Managing the risks of copyright infringement

An obvious way to avoid infringing the copyright in an existing work is not to copy it at all, though in the spirit of 'harnessing collective intelligence' cross-referral and mutual recognition is common. Bloggers should therefore be careful about how much they copy from an existing work. If they do copy a 'substantial' part (see above), they should either obtain consent from the copyright owner first or, where a fair dealing defence does apply (for example, journalistic blogging), they should ensure that they include appropriate acknowledgements. A reference to the existing work will not be a defence to copyright infringement in itself, though it may go some way to pacifying the original author, it may avoid a breach of any moral rights (see above for an explanation of moral rights) and it may help to establish a 'fair dealing' defence. They should also check the terms of use of any website they wish to take material from – these may give readers a specific right to reproduce the website contents, subject to certain restrictions.

Users of the social web should also be aware of the terms of use of their service providers, including both internet service providers (ISPs) and social website operators (see 'User contracts and terms of use' below). Service providers are likely to require a warranty that any material contributed will not infringe third-party rights; breach may result in suspension or termination of access to the service, and in some cases indemnities for any costs suffered by the service provider (for instance, if they were sued by the copyright owner).

The bloggers' guide: Protecting your rights

There are a number of steps that writers can take to protect their works. First, they should identify all of the materials likely to have copyright protection. Copyright owners should also put the public on notice that they are the owners of the rights in the works that they publish. Commonly, terms of use include a statement identifying the owner of rights in the content (see 'User contracts and terms of use' below), warning users that the copyright owner is prepared to assert these rights and creating a presumption that the stated owner is the actual owner in case of dispute.

---

7   G. Sandoval (2007) 'Prince lashes out at YouTube, eBay and The Pirate Bay', CNET News.com, http://www.news.com/8301-10784_3-9778087-7.html.

Brand Protection – Trade Marks, Passing Off and Domain Names

Contributors to the social web may use trade marks, brands or trading names, which may be protected by the law. Examples might include where an employee writes a blog complaining about their employer and identifies the employer in the blog, or a consumer complains about the quality of a seller's goods or services.

BRAND PROTECTION – THE LAW

Trading names, brand names and logos may be protected by registered trade marks. Registered trade marks provide protection in the jurisdictions where they are registered. The owner of a UK or European Community registered trade mark may stop third parties from using in the course of trade the same mark in relation to the same goods and services or, where the use is likely to confuse the public, the same mark in relation to similar goods and services or a similar mark in relation to the same or similar goods and services. This would be an infringement of the owner's registered trade mark.[8]

Rights in a name or logo may also be acquired through a period of use, where a significant reputation and goodwill has been acquired in the mark. In those cases, the owner may be able to stop third-party use of the mark if such use amounts to a misrepresentation and causes the owner damage. Unauthorized use of a mark is also known as 'passing off'.

Owners of registered or unregistered rights in a trade mark may be able to challenge another party who has registered a domain name for the same or a similar word and to require the transfer of a domain name registration to them (see below for more information).

The rights of a trade mark owner to stop use of its mark by a third party are not without limits, however. For example, it may not be infringement to refer to someone else's trade mark in comparative advertising provided that the use complies with a number of criteria, including whether the use is fair.[9] A word may also be used in text without risk of infringement if that use is simply intended to refer to the relevant goods and services but it is not 'trade mark' use (for example, if a blogger writes 'I woke up and drank a Pepsi').

---

8   Trade Marks Act 1994, Section 10.
9   Reg 5 Control of Misleading Advertisements (Amendment) Regulations 2000/914, amending the Control of Misleading Advertisements Regulations 1988.

BRAND PROTECTION AND SOCIAL MEDIA

Contributors to sites on the social web may intentionally or unintentionally include or allude to brands owned by third parties, for instance to associate themselves with the brand or to criticize the products of the brand owner. For example, MySpace members may choose to customize their home pages to include names, logos and 'get up' that is based on (or copied directly from) brand owners.

This may not cause brand owners a concern where users are neither disparaging the brand nor attempting to use it to promote their site. But when users start to generate their own revenues, brand owners are more likely to take note. For instance, when eBay users started to sell items purporting to be sourced from the brand owner, the users were successfully sued in the US for trade mark infringement.[10]

The law on trade marks does not sit comfortably within this new era of freely available commentary. Though criticism and comment may not amount to 'trade mark' use that technically infringes the owner's rights, as blogging and other social networking sites become increasingly popular – and the participants become increasingly (financially) successful – it is likely that the use of brand names and logos by users will become more heavily scrutinized by brand owners. Global brand owners can be aggressive in attempting to control the use of their brands regardless of whether users are intentionally trading off their names.

The bloggers' guide: Managing the risks of infringing rights in brands

Given the risk that a domain name could infringe a trade mark, as with any other website, anyone setting up a blog should be careful to select a domain name that is not identical to or similar to anyone else's blog, trading name or product name.

For .co.uk domain names, any person claiming rights in the name through the procedure of the UK registrar Nominet would have to prove that the registration was abusive (that is, that it took unfair advantage of their rights; http://www.nominet.org.uk/disputes/drs/policy/?contentId=3069). If such a domain name is used for a blog with no commercial or trading purpose and is used purely to post comments, a brand owner may not be able to recover the

---

10 M. Lewis (2004) 'eBay Sellers Charged With Trademark Infringement', Auctionbytes, http://www.auctionbytes.com/cab/abn/y04/m08/i23/s02.

domain name under the Nominet procedure, though this may vary in other jurisdictions (see 'Jurisdictions' below).

Also, bloggers who link to content on a third party's site from a blog should make it clear that they are not trying to pass off the content as being their own. This is particularly an issue where 'framing' of another's content appears on the blogger's own site. Best practice is to acknowledge the source of the content in, or next to, the hyperlink, and bloggers should also check the terms of use of the websites they link to.

The use of a trade mark *not* in the course of trade may not amount to trade mark infringement. Use of a name or logo in a blog merely commenting on or referring to the goods or services that are the subject of the mark is unlikely to constitute trade mark infringement (although there is as yet no case law on this point relating to blogs). As mentioned above, however, this does not necessarily mean that trade mark owners will not be aggrieved by any use and try to require a blogger to cease use. In a recent case, a US lawyer used a company's logo on his blog to report on another recent US case involving that company.[11] The US lawyer received a notice from the company requiring him to remove the logo. However, under UK law, though other rights could be infringed by the use (for example, copyright in logos), this appears to be non-'trade mark' use and accordingly it seems unlikely that it would amount to trade mark infringement.

The bloggers' guide: Protecting your own brand

Bloggers may acquire their own rights in the name of their blogs. For example, if a blogger has been writing for some time, he or she may have acquired goodwill or a reputation in the name of the blog. The blogger may therefore be able to stop others from using the blog name as the name of another blog or otherwise and from misrepresenting themselves as being linked to the blogger. It is likely that the blogger would need to be able to show some financial loss to be able to successfully claim 'passing off' in those circumstances.

Likewise, bloggers might wish to consider applying for a registered trade mark in the name of their blogs. This would help to protect the name if it is particularly important to the writers, and could enable them to stop third parties from using their names in the course of trade without consent, or from registering similar domain names in an attempt to pass themselves off as being

---

11 M. Sachoff (2007) 'Blogger Bullied to Remove Avis Logo', WebProNews, http://www. webpronews.com/topnews/2007/11/13/blogger-bullied-to-remove-avis-logo.

linked to the blogs. Owners of a registered trade mark may place a ® sign by their trade marks. Owners of unregistered trade marks can also alert the public that they are treating the mark as a trade mark (and consequently may consider enforcing their rights) by placing the letters ™ by their trade marks.

Bloggers who are worried about others linking to pages of their blog without an acknowledgement referring to their site name should consider including a provision in their site's terms of use requiring any links to acknowledge them as owner of the page (see 'User contracts and terms of use' below.)

Defamation

Put simply, the law of defamation allows individuals (but not companies) to take action if third parties make untrue derogatory statements about them.

DEFAMATION – THE LAW

What is a defamatory statement?

In order to succeed in an action for defamation in the UK, a claimant must show three things:

- **A statement is defamatory**: A defamatory statement is one that 'lower[s] the claimant in the estimation of right-thinking people generally'.[12] However, the test also contains a subjective element because the characteristics of the individual who is defamed and the people to whom the statement is made will be also be taken into consideration.[13]

- **It refers to the claimant**: This is generally not difficult to establish.

- **It has been published by the defendant to a third party**: See below for more discussion about the meaning of 'published'.

If a claimant successfully establishes these three elements, then the claim for defamation will succeed unless the defendant can demonstrate that the statement is in fact true, or that another defence applies (see below). The claimant does not generally need to show that they have suffered any loss (though this would affect the amount of any damages awarded).

---

12 *Sim v Stretch* (1936) 2 All ER 1237 at p. 1240, see also *Youssoupoff v Metro-Goldwyn-Mayer Pictures Limited* (1934) 50 TLR 581.

13 See *Loutchanksky v Times Newspapers* (2001) for an analysis of this.

The law of defamation covers defamatory statements made in speech (which, together with other transitory statements, are known as slander) and in writing (which, together with other permanent statements, are libel). It also includes statements made in the form of pictures and signs. Though there has been some debate over whether statements published on the internet are in a permanent form, the courts have tended to take the view that they are – and accordingly classified them as libel rather than slander.[14] However, the status of certain social media such as instant messaging has yet to be tested.

Who is liable?

Authors, editors and publishers of defamatory statements may all be liable.[15] 'Publishers' has a broad definition. In one old case,[16] a person was regarded as having contributed to the publication of a defamatory statement simply by making others aware of its existence (by pointing to a placard on a roadside). In the same way, a service provider on the internet could be held to contribute to a statement's publication simply by hosting it on a website.

Frequently, the person who makes a defamatory statement is hard to trace or has insufficient assets to justify bringing an action. Claimants have therefore tended to pursue the publisher (which might include an ISP or other social media service provider), in the belief that they are more likely to obtain a satisfactory remedy.

A claimant has only one year from the date of publication of a statement in which to bring an action.[17] However, in the context of statements made on the internet, this period may be extended indefinitely because the one year period starts again every time the website is re-published,[18] so a party could be liable for a defamatory statement on a website many years after it is first published.

Unless the defendant can establish a defence (see below) the claimant may be entitled to damages or an injunction to prevent publication.

The defences

Authors and publishers of defamatory comments may be able to rely on a number of defences. Typically, service providers such as ISPs will now rely on

---

14 See for example *Laurence Godfrey v Demon Internet Limited (1999) 4 All ER 342*.
15 Defamation Act 1996, Section 1.
16 *Hird v Wood* (1894) 38 SJ 234.
17 Limitation Act 1980, Section 4(a).
18 *Duke of Brunswick v Harmer* (1849) 14 Q.B. 185; *Loutchansky v Times Newspapers Limited (2001)*.

the exemptions under the UK's e-Commerce Regulations[19] (see 'E-commerce and the "hosting" exemption' below). Authors and service providers may also be able to rely on the following defences:

- **Innocent dissemination:** The publisher has no knowledge or control over the defamatory statement (see below for more details).

- **Justification:** Showing that the statement was true.

- **Fair comment on a matter of public interest:** Provided that the statement was made with the belief that the comment was true.

- **Privilege:** May include circumstances where the publication of the statement was in the public interest.[20]

Users who write defamatory statements are unlikely to be able to rely on the 'innocent dissemination' defence, though the defences of 'justification', 'fair comment' and 'privilege' may be available. Service providers are less likely to rely on the latter three defences (because they will publish the defamatory statement but not necessarily know whether the statement was true, fair comment or in the public interest). However, they may be able to rely on the 'innocent dissemination' defence if they:[21]

- are not the author, editor or publisher;

- take reasonable care in the statement's publication; and

- did not know nor had reason to believe that what they did caused or contributed to the publication of a defamatory statement.

An author is, as the name suggests, the original source of the defamatory statement, an editor is a person having editorial responsibility in relation to a statement and a publisher is a commercial publisher who issues material containing the statement in the course of its business.[22]

An entity will specifically not be considered to fall within the category of author, editor or publisher if it is only:

- involved in processing, making copies of or distributing or selling any electronic medium in or on which the statement is recorded;

19 Electronic Commerce (EC Directive) Regulations 2002.
20 *Reynolds v Times Newspapers* (1999) 3WLR 1010.
21 Defamation Act 1996, Section 1.
22 Defamation Act 1996, Section 1(2).

- the operator or provider of a system or service by which the statement is available in electronic form; or

- the operator of or provider of a communications system by the means of which the statement is transmitted or made available by a person over whom the owner has no effective control.

This test should generally provide protection for ISPs and other service providers, as long as they take reasonable care (see above), though it is not yet clear precisely what 'reasonable care' means in this context. Would it include, for instance, random content checks? Generally, the courts' approach to this issue has depended on the circumstances of the publication.

In Godfrey v Demon Internet,[23] a defamatory statement was posted about Laurence Godfrey on a forum hosted by Demon internet (an ISP). Godfrey faxed Demon asking it to remove the statement. Demon did not act on this request for 10 days. The court held that Demon could not rely on the innocent dissemination defence because it was a publisher, it had not taken care in relation to the statement's publication (in that it failed to act quickly to remove it) and it knew of its existence.

Contrast this with the recent John Bunt[24] case, where the extent of the defendant's knowledge (or lack of in this case) was key. If a defendant did not know nor had reason to suspect they were assisting with the publication of a defamatory statement then they would be likely to be able to rely on the defence.

DEFAMATION AND SOCIAL MEDIA

The law of defamation may affect users and service providers on the social web. Users may be authors or editors of defamatory statements, which may include images submitted to photograph sharing sites such as Flickr and videos submitted to YouTube. For instance, in 2002 a teacher won damages from an ex-pupil who had posted defamatory comments about him on Friends Reunited,[25] and in 2007 another teacher won an action against a pupil in Finland for posting a defamatory video to YouTube.[26] Interestingly, in both cases the claimant chose to sue the individual rather than the (considerably richer) publisher.

---

23 *Laurence Godfrey v Demon Internet Limited* (1999) 4 All ER 342.
24 *John Bunt v David Tilley and others* (2006) EWCH 407 (QB).
25 Case in the small claims court – see J. Leyden (2002) 'Friends Reunited user in libel payout', The Register, http://www.theregister.co.uk/2002/05/21/friends_reunited_user_in_libel/.
26 Jaani.net (2007) 'Plaintiff Wins YouTube Defamation Action', http://www.jaani.net/view/2007/08/26/you-tube-defamation-action.

Service providers may be publishers of defamatory comments made by bloggers, contributors to wikis or members of networking groups. They may be editors, for instance if they moderate posts made to a forum. Accordingly, service providers may also be liable where they do not act to remove allegedly defamatory material that is posted to their websites.

Service providers may also be required by the courts to disclose personal details about any users who post defamatory content. See 'Privacy and data protection' below for details about a recent case involving allegedly defamatory comments made on a forum about the directors of a football club in which the court balanced the merits of ordering disclosure against the forum's obligations under the Data Protection Act.

The bloggers' guide: Managing the risks of defamation

Users of the social web should be aware that any comments they make about third parties that are published – whether on social networking sites, discussion boards, blogs or otherwise – are subject to the usual laws of defamation. They should avoid making statements that may be defamatory – such as any unsubstantiated criticism of third parties. They should also be aware of their obligations under the terms of use imposed by their service providers. It is likely that they will be asked to warrant that the information they submit is not defamatory. See 'User contracts and terms of use' below for more information about terms of use.

Service providers should consider ways to manage their risks. Common practice is to follow a 'notice and take down' procedure – that is, to act quickly to remove information on receipt of notice that it may be defamatory. Clearly, this needs to be weighed against the service providers' relationship with its users, contractual and otherwise. Commonly, service providers choose to remove the statement, notify the author and then sometimes commence an internal dispute mechanism engaged to allow the author to put their views across. Other service providers simply remove any allegedly defamatory material without further checks, to save resources. Service providers should accordingly consider including in their terms of use the right to remove information at any time without notice where they have reason to suspect content may breach the terms of use.

Privacy and Data Protection

DATA PROTECTION – THE LAW

The UK's Data Protection Act 1998, implementing the EU's Data Protection Directive,[27] regulates the processing of personal data within the UK. Under the Act, 'personal data' means information identifying living individuals that is held on computers and certain manual files (including information collected through websites); and 'processing' essentially covers doing anything with the data (for example, collecting, holding, using, modifying or deleting the data). The Act imposes obligations on the 'data controllers' of that data (that is, the parties determining how and why the data are processed).

The Act requires data controllers to comply with eight data protection principles when processing personal data. These require the data to be:[28]

- fairly and lawfully processed;
- processed for limited purposes;
- adequate, relevant and not excessive;
- accurate and up to date;
- not kept for longer than is necessary;
- processed in line with the rights of the individuals;
- secure; and
- not transferred to other countries without adequate protection.

The requirement of the first principle to process personal data 'fairly and lawfully' includes an obligation to notify individuals, generally when their data are collected, of the identity of the data controller, the purposes for which their data will be processed (in particular anything that is not obvious), and any other information required to make the processing fair. Data controllers on the web generally seek to comply with this obligation by including statements containing the key information at the point that the data are collected (typically on web forms) and more detail about data processing in their privacy policies. The information provided at the point of collection should also include any

---

27 Directive 95/46/EC 'on the Protection of Individuals with regard to the Processing of Personal Data'.
28 Data Protection Act 1998, Schedule 1.

anticipated disclosures of the data, which may include transfers to third parties or publication on websites.

So, for example, where users register to use a discussion board, the operator of the discussion board will generally determine how and why the users' data is to be processed and accordingly be the 'data controller' of the data of its users. The operator should identify itself and inform users what their data will be used for when they first submit their details. The second principle stops the website operator from using users' data for any other purposes.

The third, fourth and fifth principles govern the procedures for maintaining data quality, for instance stopping data controllers from holding personal data 'just in case' they might find a use for it in future (the data must not be excessive), or from holding it any longer than necessary. These principles also require data controllers to take steps to ensure that the data remains accurate and up to date, which might include periodically asking individuals to check their details.

The sixth principle (processing in line with individuals' rights) requires data controllers to comply with certain rights of the individuals, for instance giving them the right to access their data and to object to processing for direct marketing purposes.

The seventh principle covers the data controllers' security obligations, including technical (which may, depending on the nature of the data, include using secure network connections, encryption and passwords) and operational (which might mean training employees about the Act). It also requires data controllers to put in place suitable written contracts where they transfer personal data to third-party 'data processors' who carry out processing activities on their behalf (for example, mailing houses for sending direct marketing literature).

The eighth principle means that data controllers can not transfer personal data outside the European Economic Area (that is, the EU plus Iceland, Liechtenstein and Norway) without ensuring adequate protection for the rights and freedoms of the individuals whose data are to be transferred. There are a limited number of ways of achieving this, including putting in place suitable contracts with the recipients, obtaining the consent of the data subject, and carrying out full due diligence checks on the country and recipient in question. The European Court of Justice has held that simply publishing personal data on a website in the EU will not of itself amount to a transfer outside the EEA.[29]

---

29 *Lindqvist v Kammaraklagaren* ECJ Case C-101/01, November 6, 2003.

There are exemptions from the requirements of the Act where data are processed for purely domestic purposes. However, this exemption will generally not apply where the data are published on the internet.[30]

Data controllers that breach the Act may be investigated by the Information Commissioner, the UK regulator for data protection. The Information Commissioner may issue enforcement notices requiring data controllers to comply with the Act; failure to comply with an enforcement notice is a criminal offence. There have been discussions in the UK about increasing the Information Commissioner's enforcement powers but for now there remains a perception that the biggest risk of non-compliance with the Act is of bad publicity for the data controller.

PRIVACY AND CONFIDENCE – THE LAW

Following the recent decisions in the Campbell[31] and Hello![32] cases, there is also a developing area of law around individuals' rights to privacy and use of their image under the existing law of confidence. The law of confidence protects confidential information (for example, a trade secret) that has been disclosed in circumstances giving rise to an obligation to respect the confidentiality of the information (for example, under a confidentiality agreement). A disclosure may be justified where the public interest outweighs the discloser's right for the information to remain confidential.

The discloser of the confidential information may be entitled to an injunction to prevent disclosure and/or damages if there is a breach by the recipient causing loss.

In the Campbell case, the court applied the existing law of confidence to disclosures of personal information relating to individuals' private lives. In applying the public interest test, the court balanced the right to privacy under Article 8 of the Human Rights Act with the discloser's right to freedom of expression under Article 10.

PRIVACY AND SOCIAL MEDIA

The social web is by its nature rich in personal data, ranging from information identifying the authors of blog and forum posts and comments to the vast aggregation of personal details, photographs and videos accumulating on

---

30 *Lindqvist v Kammaraklagaren* ECJ Case C-101/01, November 6, 2003.
31 *Campbell v MGN* (2004) UKHL 22.
32 *Douglas and another and others v Hello! Ltd and others* (2007) UKHL 21.

social networking websites such as LinkedIn, MySpace and Facebook. This has also led to debate about achieving an appropriate balance between the right of Web 2.0 businesses to exploit the data they are collecting and rights of the individual users (for example, under the Data Protection Act and the law of confidence).[33]

Generally, the operator of a website on the social web based in the UK will act as a data controller of the information it collects and consequently have to comply with the eight data protection principles. Even Facebook (http://www.facebook.com/policy.php) and MySpace (http://collect.myspace.com/misc/privacy.html), albeit that they may not be subject to the UK's Data Protection Act if they do not have offices or processing activities in the UK, set out in their privacy policies details of what information they collect, what they will do with the information, and what disclosures they may make.

Concern has been expressed where users submit personal data relating to third parties, for instance photographs of their friends and family that users submit to social networking sites or photo sharing sites such as Flickr, when those third parties may not themselves have agreed to the service provider's terms of use. Who is the data controller in this instance? The service provider may argue that they do not determine how or why this third-party data is processed and, accordingly, that they are not data controllers. Facebook attempts to manage the risk by requiring users to warrant that the content they submit will not 'violate or infringe upon the rights of any third party, including ... privacy, publicity or other personal or proprietary rights' (http://www.facebook.com/terms.php).

Another issue for social web service providers occurs where third parties request access to the personal data they hold. Users of the social web often operate under an assumption of anonymity on the basis that their details will not be published when they post. However, recent cases have made clear that where users post defamatory material to forums or share material that infringes copyright, claimants can make successful requests to the ISPs or website operators for disclosure of the users' identities,[34] allowing claimants to sue the users.

---

33 See, for example, R. Blakely (2007) 'Does Facebook's privacy policy stack up?', TimesOnline, http://business.timesonline.co.uk/tol/business/industry_sectors/technology/article2430927.ece.

34 Using the principles established in Norwich Pharmacal Co. v The Commissioners of Customs and Excise (1974) RPC 101, applied to the web in Totalise Plc v Motley Fool Ltd (2001) 1 P & T 764.

Contributors to a fans' website for UK soccer club Sheffield Wednesday FC criticized directors of the club; the court found that some of them had overstepped the line and made potentially defamatory comments and ordered the website operator to disclose the users' details.[35] The British Phonographic Industry also obtained from ISPs the details of users of peer-to-peer networks to allow their members to sue for copyright infringement.[36] Before ordering disclosure, the courts gave consideration to the service providers' obligations under the Data Protection Act, and balanced the rights and freedoms of the users against the legitimate interests of the service provider in making the disclosure.

The bloggers' guide: Managing privacy risks

Users of the social web should be aware of their rights and pay close attention to the terms of use and privacy policies of websites before disclosing their data, and keep their eyes out for potential changes in use by service providers. In late 2007, criticism from Facebook users over its introduction of the 'Facebook Beacon' application forced one of its founders into a public apology.[37] The application allowed Facebook to collect information about its users' spending habits on certain other websites and make it available on their Facebook profile. The application initially applied by default unless users opted out. In this instance, users' complaints led Facebook to change its policy so that the application would only apply where users gave prior consent by opting in.

Many service providers are based in countries that have a lower standard of data protection than the UK and full information about the proposed uses of the personal data may not always be displayed during the registration process.

Similarly, service providers need to think carefully about why they are collecting data and whether they can justify their use of the data, to be conscious of their obligations to notify users about the uses of their data, to put in place procedures to keep the information accurate and up to date and to respond to requests for access to the information.

Employment and Blogging

Blogging and the use of the social web can seriously damage the relationship between employer and employee. Indeed, in certain circumstances employers

---

35 Sheffield Wednesday Football Club Ltd and Others v Hargreaves (2007) EWHC 2375 (QB).
36 Polydor Limited & Others v Brown & Others (2005) EWHC 3191 (Ch).
37 M. Zuckerberg (2007) 'Thoughts on Beacon', The Facebook Blog, http://blog.facebook.com/blog.php?post=7584397130.

can lawfully dismiss an employee for the content of their blog or their use of social networking sites.

We do not have to look far for evidence of 'doocing', the online term for being sacked by one's employer as a result of a personal blog. The term appears to originate from Heather Armstrong, an American web designer who was dismissed for posting unflattering comments about colleagues in 2001.[38]

Famous casualties of doocing include Joe Gordon,[39] who allegedly made inappropriate references to his employer Waterstones in his online newsletter (http://www.woolamaloo.org.uk/) and Ellen Simonetti, a flight attendant for Delta Airlines, who was dismissed after posting 'inappropriate' photos[40] of herself wearing her uniform.[41]

This section will look at the legality of employers taking disciplinary action against employees over the content of their web presence, with a particular focus on unfair dismissal. It will also suggest ways in which both employers and employees can avoid the use of the social web impinging on the employment relationship.

It is important to note that this is an area of the law that is still developing. Although we can apply established employment law principles to the issues that new technology raises, each case will be unique. The legality of any action taken by an employer must be determined on its own facts and it is difficult to provide hard and fast rules.

Employment and Blogging – The Law

As a business or service provider, the employer will have its own interests to protect as well as those of its staff and clients. If an employee's use of the social web is considered unreasonable or inappropriate (whether inside or outside work), employers are entitled to discipline and dismiss in accordance with their internal procedures, provided that any action is fair, proportionate and lawful.

---

38   Heather Armstrong's website is http://www.dooce.com.
39   P. Barkham (2005) 'Blogger sacked for sounding off', *The Guardian*, 12 January, http://www. guardian.co.uk/technology/2005/jan/12/books.newmedia.
40   E. Simonetti (2004) 'It's over', Diary of Human Being, http://queenofsky.journalspace.com/ ?cmd=displaycomments&dcid=393&entryid=393.
41   Wikipedia (2008) 'Ellen Simonetti', http://en.wikipedia.org/wiki/Ellen_Simonetti.

The rules that regulate the employment relationship and the disciplining of employees derive from:

- the contract between employer and employee;

- the employer's own policies and procedures;

- legislation and statutory guidance; and

- case law.

EMPLOYMENT AND BLOGGING – THE LAW ON DISMISSAL

Legislation protects employees from being unfairly dismissed.[42] In the majority of cases an employee needs to have at least one year's continuous service with an employer to bring this claim.[43]

In order to dismiss fairly an employer must:

- have a potentially fair reason for dismissal;

- follow a fair procedure; and

- act reasonably in the circumstances.

Dismissal – fair reason

There are currently six potentially fair reasons for dismissal set out in legislation.[44] The most likely permitted reason that an employer may rely on in dismissing an employee for use of the social web is on the grounds of misconduct or 'some other substantial reason of a kind such as to justify the dismissal of an employee holding the position which that employee held'. The latter is very broad and is likely to be used where an employee has not committed an act of misconduct but nevertheless their continued employment is deemed untenable.

Some activities of employees will clearly be seen as potential disciplinary offences. Examples would be where an employee is using paid working time to

---

42 Employment Rights Act 1996, Section 94.
43 No qualifying service is needed for certain dismissals connected with an employee asserting certain statutory employment rights, connected to maternity, paternity or parental rights; for 'whistle blowing' under relevant legislation; and connected to certain types of trade union membership or activity; and certain issues related to health and safety. Such dismissals will be automatically unfair.
44 These are currently dismissals relating to conduct, capability, redundancy, retirement, illegality and 'some other substantial reason'. Employment Rights Act 1996, Section 98.

engage in their own online activity in breach of the employer's policy, or where they breach their employer's confidentiality online.

A trickier area is where an employer seeks to discipline an employee for online activity that is carried out outside of the work context or is not directly related to the employee's day-to-day job.

An employee's web presence, even if created in the employee's own time, can give rise to a lawful dismissal where the content is considered particularly disparaging or damaging either to the company, staff or clients. The employer may take the view that the employee has committed an act of misconduct or that the relationship of trust and confidence has broken down. So, where a blogger wishes to imply that their employer is a 'bastard' or refer to a colleague as the 'evil boss', such as in a recent case, the employee is putting themselves at significant risk of dismissal.

However, each case will be dependent on its facts and, although decided under French jurisdiction, the case of 'petite anglaise' shows that employers may not able to dismiss simply because they do not like the content of the blog. Catherine Sanderson blogged under the name of 'la petite anglaise'. She recounted tales of her love life and working for a British firm in Paris.[45] She did not mention her firm by name but her employer considered that it could be identified through photographs which Ms Sanderson had posted of herself. A French industrial tribunal did not agree, found that the dismissal was without 'real and serious cause' and awarded her a year's salary plus costs.[46]

Even if it does not directly bring the employer into disrepute, the employer may reasonably consider the employee's activities as being incompatible with the position that the employee holds. So, a dismissal was fair where a Probation Officer was dismissed by Lancashire Probation Service in the UK for selling bondage, domination and sado-masochism articles through a website.[47] The employer considered, amongst other things, that this was inconsistent with the duties of a probation officer dealing with victims of sex crimes. The tribunal stated: 'A Probation Officer like other professional people did not cease to be a Probation Officer outside hours of work. Such persons had a reputation to maintain'.[48]

---

45 http://www.petiteanglaise.com.
46 This is a French case decided under French law, but it is arguable the Employment Tribunal would take a similar approach.
47 Pay v Lancashire Probation Service (2004) ICR 187.
48 It was also found by the Employment Appeal Tribunal at a later hearing that the employee's right to a private life under the ECHR had not been breached in this case.

However, dismissing an employee for the same reasons as the above case will not necessarily be fair if carried out by another employer. The context of the employment is important and in these types of cases it is notoriously difficult to show that the employment and the extra curricular activities are incompatible. Dismissals connected with activities outside work need to be handled very carefully.

Dismissal – procedure

In addition to having a fair reason for dismissal, the employer must follow a fair procedure. When conducting any disciplinary or dismissal process in the UK, the ACAS guidance on disciplinary procedures (http://www.acas.org.uk) should be considered alongside the employer's own disciplinary procedures. When looking at whether dismissal is fair, an employment tribunal will consider the employer's own policies, guidance from ACAS and the principles of natural justice (that is, whether the employee was given a fair hearing in front of an impartial person).

At the time of writing, statutory dismissal and disciplinary procedures,[49] apply where the employer contemplates dismissing an employee or taking relevant disciplinary action against them. These include, amongst other things, the requirement of a right of appeal against dismissal. If these statutory procedures are not followed the dismissal will be automatically unfair.

Dismissal – overall reasonableness

In addition to establishing a fair reason and procedure, the dismissal must be reasonable in the circumstances. For example, before dismissing, an employer should consider whether dismissal is consistent with disciplinary sanctions for other offences, the employee's length of service and any mitigation the employee put forward (such as having no previous misconduct or offering to remove the offending material).

The courts have held that there are a range of reasonable responses that an employer might take when dealing with a possible dismissal. If the decision to dismiss is one which a reasonable employer *could* take, the dismissal will be fair.

If an employer has clear guidelines and policies detailing what may be inappropriate online behaviour, and the employee was fully aware of them, it will be easier to show that the dismissal was reasonable.

---

49 The Employment Act 2002 (Dispute Resolution) Regulations 2004 (SI 2004/752), see also ACAS guidance (http://www.acas.org.uk).

EMPLOYMENT AND BLOGGING – THE LAW ON DISCRIMINATION

Employers should be aware of the impact of anti-discrimination legislation when considering taking action against employees over the contents of their blog or out-of-work activities. Currently discrimination is prohibited on the grounds of:

- sex (includes marital status and gender reassignment)

- race (includes, colour, nationality, ethnic or national origins)

- disability

- sexual orientation (includes heterosexuality, homosexuality and bisexuality)[50]

- religion

- age.

Employers should take care that their standards of what is or is not acceptable for employees to publish on the web are not influenced by prejudices that may amount to discrimination. In some cases discrimination can be justified, but this is rare.

Employers may be held responsible (or 'vicariously liable') for acts of discrimination or harassment committed by an employee towards third parties. So, for example, if one employee sexually harasses another, the employer can be ordered to pay compensation. The law on employer's responsibilities can be complex, particularly if the harassment occurs outside the course of the employee's employment. However, employers should take reasonable steps to prevent the harassment or discrimination occurring through the use of the social web in the workplace. Steps might include linking an equal opportunities policy with an internet use policy and ensuring staff and managers receive appropriate training, and handling any complaints effectively.

EMPLOYMENT AND BLOGGING – THE LAW'S REMEDIES

If an employee believes they have been dismissed unfairly because of their use of the social web or otherwise, they may bring proceedings in the employment

---

50 It does not include particular sexual practices or fetishes so, for example, neither sado-masochism nor paedophilia is protected.

tribunal and claim compensation for financial loss that they have suffered as a result of the dismissal.[51]

If the employee can successfully show that the employer's disciplinary action or other detriment amounted to an act of discrimination then compensation can be unlimited (although it is still based on the employee's loss) and an award for injury to feelings can be made.

Aside from financial implications, employers need to consider the potentially damaging publicity associated with a successful claim arising from this type of dismissal.

EMPLOYMENT AND SOCIAL MEDIA

As we have discussed above, the advent of social media has provided new opportunities for employees, but also brought new challenges for employers wishing to manage their own risks without unduly restricting their staff. We consider below some of the ways that employers can do so.

The bloggers' guide: Managing the risks for employers

In order to ensure that bloggers know what is expected of them, employers are advised to have clear and well-drafted policies covering what is (or is not) acceptable behaviour in relation to their use of the social web both inside and outside work. For example, an employer may wish to state that employees should not publish information about their employer or colleagues without prior permission.

Policies should cover the use of the internet during work time and list (non-exhaustively) what may be considered misconduct in relation to the employer's activities on the web. These policies should ideally cross-refer to disciplinary and equal opportunities policies.

If employers do not wish employees to use the employer's facilities for personal use this should be clearly communicated to the employee. If employers allow limited use inside work, the boundaries of that use must also be clearly stated. Employers could consider limiting personal use to outside core hours and blocking social websites.

---

51   The maximum amount of the compensation award is set annually. From February 2008 this is £63,000. Most employment disputes are litigated in the employment tribunal, although some employees may bring a claim in the civil courts especially for larger breach of contract claims.

Note that issues may arise in respect of monitoring of employees' web use at work. These will include rights under the Data Protection Act 1998 and the Regulation of Investigatory Powers Act 2000 and are outside the scope of this chapter. Employers should be aware of the Information Commissioner's The Employment Practices Data Protection Code: Part 3 (http://www.ico.gov.uk) which sets out best practice in this area.

All policies should be brought clearly to the attention on employees. If policies are not in place, disciplinary action can still occur, but it may be more difficult to show that the employer's actions were reasonable.

The bloggers' guide: Reducing the risks for employees

Bloggers should take account of their employer's views, perceived reputation and ethos and, in relation to that, how their employer would consider their blog or web presence. An employer may not be able to dictate what a blogger writes, but the reality is that an employer has the power to dismiss an employee (whether fairly or otherwise) if they do not agree with a blog's contents. In terms of blogging about work, the best advice must surely come from Heather Armstrong, the original 'doocee':

> My advice to you is be ye not so stupid. Never write about work on the internet unless your boss knows and sanctions the fact that you are writing about work on the internet.[52]

E-Commerce and the 'Hosting' Exemption

E-COMMERCE EXEMPTIONS – THE LAW

Since 2002, ISPs and other service providers in the UK have been entitled to rely on certain defences under the e-Commerce Regulations[53] to claims of intellectual property infringement, defamation and other civil and criminal claims. These defences do not apply to individuals responsible for creating the content. They provide for exemption from liability where entities are acting as 'mere conduits', and where they are merely caching or hosting content in each case provided that the service providers meet certain criteria (see below).

---

52 From Heather Armstrong's website, http://www.dooce.com.
53 Electronic Commerce (EC Directive) Regulations 2002.

E-COMMERCE EXEMPTIONS AND SOCIAL MEDIA

Unlike ISPs, service providers operating websites on the social web are unlikely to be able to rely on the mere conduit or caching defences because content will often be stored permanently. However, the hosting exemption may still apply.

The bloggers' guide: Relying on the hosting exemption

Service providers will only be able to rely on the hosting exemption in relation to any claim if they do not know that the relevant content is unlawful and they act 'expeditiously' to remove or disable access to the content on receipt of notice of the nature of the content. We discussed in 'Privacy and data protection' above the way that service providers often apply a 'notice and take down' procedure to manage the risk of defamation claims, and similar principles apply here.

The courts have not yet fully explored what acting 'expeditiously' requires or the precise scope of what constitutes notice of unlawful content, and this is likely to depend on the circumstances. For instance, if a service provider receives notice about a class of illegal content, does the service provider have an obligation to take steps to identify any specific items that fall within the class?

The exemption does raise another question: should service providers (including people running blogs that facilitate comment) check for illegal content and/or moderate content? There is no statutory obligation on web hosts to check all hosted material, and if content is checked, a web site host will be deemed to be aware of it and may no longer have the benefit of protection under the e-Commerce Regulations. However, if content is not reviewed, users might upload content that is wholly inappropriate to major sites hosted by the web host, and this could be available for some time without any action to remove it, and could have consequences for the service provider's goodwill.

The appropriate choice will depend on the volume of the content in question, the user base and the resources available to the web host. A prudent middle ground may be to use software tools to monitor unusual activity within web space, such as a spike of traffic relating to a specific file or files, and then to examine those particular files.

User Contracts and Terms of Use

Website terms of use are essentially a contract between the website owner and its users. They are generally intended to protect the intellectual property rights of the website owner and to limit its liability for claims from users and other third parties.

TERMS OF USE – THE LAW

For website terms of use to form a valid and enforceable contract between the website owner and its users, under English law, users need to agree to the terms. Ideally this would be explicit, for example, by requiring users to confirm they have read and accepted the terms upon registering on the site or by clicking an 'I Agree' button.

However, while this works well where users need to register in order to use the site, where websites are not interactive (for example, where users read blogs but do not post any comments) this is generally not an option. Therefore, the website owner will need to rely on implied acceptance by users by virtue of having had an opportunity to read the terms. In reality, this means having a link to the website terms at least on the homepage of the site and preferably on every page. Ideally, this should be positioned prominently so that users are likely to see it without scrolling (even if generally few will actually read the terms in full). This is standard practice on many websites, but whether it actually results in a contract between the website owner and user, on which either of them can rely, has yet to be tested in an English court.

TERMS OF USE AND SOCIAL MEDIA

Any social website, be it a networking site, wiki, discussion forum or other site that encourages contributions by third parties, would be advised to have terms of use to manage the risks and protect the rights of its owners. However, even individuals should at least consider a short form version for their private blogs.

The bloggers' guide: Understanding terms of use

Terms of use will typically do some or all of the following:

- State who owns the intellectual property rights in the website (see 'Copyright' and 'Brand protection – trade marks, passing off and domain names' above). While such a statement does not change the position on legal ownership, it puts third parties on notice of the asserted ownership of rights and creates a presumption that the stated owner is the actual owner.

- Specify what users can and cannot do with the website's content. It is common to permit users to download and use content for their personal use (or perhaps internal business purposes). There are usually restrictions on further copying and distribution, particularly for commercial gain. Without specifically stating what users can and cannot do, it is likely to be much harder to prevent unwanted use of the site and its content, and the scope of a user's rights will be uncertain.

- Require users to give warranties about their use of the website, for instance that they will not disrupt the use of the website by other users (for example, sending spam or denial of service attacks), upload defamatory, abusive or other illegal content or anything that infringes the rights of other people, hack into the site or transmit viruses to the server hosting the site.

- Require users to keep any usernames and passwords confidential and restrict misuse or sharing of login details.

- Disclaim liability for third-party sites that are linked to or from the website, given that the website owner will generally have no control over unrelated sites. This may be less appropriate (and is potentially unenforceable) if linked sites are part of the same group of sites, under common control or are specifically endorsed or approved by the website owner.

- Limit or exclude liability for any loss or damage resulting from use of the site or reliance on its contents. Under English law, there are restrictions on the ability to limit or exclude liability, and any attempts to do so may be unenforceable if a court decides they are unreasonable or unfair. If a social website is aimed at particularly sensitive matters such as health or child-related issues or provides advice that, if wrong or if used incorrectly, could result in personal injury or damage to property, the writers should consider the disclaimers and limitations on liability in their terms of use even more carefully and would be well advised to seek professional advice.

- Specify which laws will govern the terms of use and which courts will determine any disputes relating to the website. For website owners based in England and Wales (or for sites specifically targeted at the UK), it is standard practice to choose English law and the English courts. However, given the global nature of the internet, it is not possible in all cases to avoid the laws of other countries. Where UK-based sites are specifically aimed at other jurisdictions, in particular sites selling goods or services, site owners should consider taking separate advice in the relevant countries.

- Identify some of the consequences of breach of the terms of use – for example, suspension or termination of access to the site, disclosure of information to third parties (for instance following allegations that users have contributed unlawful content), or potentially indemnities for any losses suffered by the service provider (though this may be of little value against an individual user with limited assets).

In conjunction with its terms of use, social websites will generally use a privacy policy dealing with their handling of personal data provided by users that register on the site (see 'Privacy and data protection' below).

While the jury is still out on the effectiveness of terms of use in protecting website owners from liability, the explosion of social networking and other cooperative websites means that those that run them are dealing with greater numbers of users (and contributors) than ever. Some risk of liability is inevitable as in most fields, but terms of use are an easy way of attempting to manage this. However, service providers and website owners need to note that there is no guarantee that such steps will prevent them being liable for content, and in high-risk areas such as the provision of health advice, it would be prudent to seek insurance cover against such liability.

Jurisdiction

This chapter has focused on the key issues under the laws of England and Wales for users of the social web. While it is outside the scope of this chapter to consider the laws applying outside of England and Wales, users and service providers should be aware that they may be liable in other jurisdictions for breaches of the law, depending on the circumstances in which they make content available. This will depend on the possible breach and the jurisdiction in question.

For instance, in defamation, the position in common law countries is that publication takes the place where the content is read, heard or seen, and not where the material was first placed on the internet.[54]

The courts in these jurisdictions have resisted attempts by content publishers to limit their liability by directing or targeting publications to certain jurisdictions. This is likely to mean that provided a claimant can show that publication has occurred in England and Wales and the claimant has a reputation here, courts in England and Wales are likely to be willing to hear a defamation case whether or not a defendant is based here.

The position other countries would take to hear claims based on allegedly defamatory statements published in their jurisdiction is outside the scope of this chapter, as it is dependent on national laws on defamation and cross-jurisdictional claims.

Summing Up – Other Issues and the Future

We have focused on some of the key areas of development in the regulation of the social web. However, this chapter is by no means comprehensive and a number of other UK laws may also apply to users and service providers. For instance:

- **Obscenity and indecency**: There are laws restricting the publication of certain categories of material, such as obscene material that tends to 'deprave and corrupt'.[55]

- **Harassment and cyber-bullying**: Under both specific legislation addressing the internet and the general laws on harassment.[56]

- **Incitement offences**: Including content that incites racial and potentially religious hatred, as well as content that incites or glorifies terrorism.[57]

- **Regulation of direct marketing**: In addition to the data protection issues discussed in 'Privacy and data protection' above, the sending

---

54 Gutnick v Dow Jones & Co Inc (2001) 2 All E.R. 986 and Harrods Ltd v Dow Jones & Co Inc (2003) EWHC 1162.
55 Obscene Publications Act 1959, Section 1; see also Protection of Children Act 1978, the Indecent Displays (Controls) Act 1981, and the Sexual Offences Act 2003.
56 See, for example, Communications Act 2003, Section 127 .
57 Terrorism Acts 2000 and 2006.

of direct marketing information by email is regulated by the Privacy and e-Communications Regulations.[58]

- **Discrimination**: There are laws governing discrimination on the basis of sex, race, age, disability and sexual orientation and the laws on disability require website operators to take certain steps to make their services available to disabled users.

- **Other intellectual property rights**: As well as copyright and trade marks, other intellectual property rights may be relevant, such as database rights, design rights and patents.

As we have seen, the laws applying to the social web are varied and in places complex, particularly as users, service providers and the courts strive to understand the impact of technologies and activities that were not envisaged when the majority of the existing laws were conceived or drafted.

For users of the social web, the key advice from this chapter is to consider the risks carefully before posting, uploading, commenting, editing or publishing. The social web has empowered its user-participants – but it has also exposed them to unfamiliar risks and potential liabilities. Users would do well to bear in mind the advice Uncle Ben gave to Peter Parker in the film *Spider-Man*:

Remember, with great power, comes great responsibility.[59]

---

58 Privacy and Electronic Communications (EC Directive) Regulations 2003.
59 IMDb (2002) 'Memorable quotes for Spider-Man', http://www.imdb.com/title/tt0145487/quotes.

Online Reputation

The social web can have a massive impact on reputation, whether you like it or not, and whether we're talking about business or personal reputation.

With the web, opinions, facts, truth and lies can spread across the world as fast as a rumour or piece of gossip might have passed amongst the inhabitants of a small town 100 years ago. In the case of a town, the size would tend to limit the number of people who might receive the information, and (unless particularly exciting) the information would not pass beyond the edges of the town. With the internet, those communication barriers do not exist; the only barrier (and it is a weak one) is language. In the first part of this chapter, we will consider how to go about monitoring, enhancing and protecting your online reputation, be it your personal reputation or that of your business.

There has for a long time been a degree of interaction and mingling between reputation – the world or PR – and the law. To take an important example that began evolving long before Tim Berners-Lee invented the worldwide web, the laws of slander and libel. With the social web, reputation and the use of legal remedies become even more closely linked. In the second part of this chapter, we look at the 'court of PR' – how social media can impact on or be used in litigation.

The 'Court of PR': Online Reputation

In terms of protecting and improving reputation, social media presents new opportunities and challenges for businesses. Whilst the opportunities will only present themselves to those businesses that become actively involved in the social web, the challenges exist for these more active businesses and those that ignore social media, whether through choice or ignorance.

For example, social media analysts have argued that blogging has a direct influence on corporate reputation.[1] The analysts, Market Sentinel, Onalytica and Immediate Future PR, produced a 'white paper' on the subject.[2] The paper focused on the example of blogger Jeff Jarvis's criticism of the computer retailer, Dell. It argued that Dell suffered long-term damage to its reputation because of the activities of bloggers. 'Bloggers have extended their influence from dominating negative perceptions of Dell to dominating perceptions of Dell's entire reputation in the customer services area', Flemming Madsen from Onalytica has been quoted as saying.

The opportunities and challenges faced by Dell are opportunities and challenges faced by all businesses. We are in an age where people increasingly go online to find new suppliers rather than using business directories such as the Yellow Pages, something born out by the statistics regularly pumped out in the IT media about the exponential growth in the number of internet users, and the number of searches performed per day. Therefore, the opportunities and threats we discuss below are relevant to organizations of all types.

MONITORING ONLINE REPUTATION

With the social web, business brand and reputation can no longer be as controlled by the efforts of the business itself. In past times, a customer wanting to tell others about their experience with a supplier would only be able to tell so many people through word of mouth, so reputation (good or bad) spread slowly. Now, customers can and often will use social media to tell others about their dealings with a business. These online communications can be anything from a few comments to even a full-scale campaign against a business.

What others say about your business online can have a big impact. Online monitoring company Marketing Sentinel found in a survey of the UK top 50 marketing brands that 40 per cent had negative or critical commentary in the top 10 Google search results.[3]

---

1   Immediate Future (2005) '"Dell Hell" blogs have measurable, long-term, negative impact on Dell's reputation: says new white paper', Responsesource, http://www.responsesource.com/releases/rel_display.php?relid=23613&hilite=.
2   Market Sentinel, Onalytica and Immediate Future PR (2005) 'Measuring the influence of bloggers on corporate reputation', http://66.102.9.104/search?q=cache:vNLv-owiefEJ:www.marketsentinel.com/files/MeasuringBloggerInfluence61205.pdf+The+analysts,+Market+Sentinel,+Onalytica+and+Immediate+Future+PR,&hl=en&ct=clnk&cd=1&gl=uk.
3   Market Sentinel and Weboptimiser (2005) 'Search is a brand', http://www.marketsentinel.com/files/Searchisbrand280605.pdf.

Whether comments and feedback are good or bad, you will not know what is being said online about you unless you somehow keep an eye on the online world. This is something you can do yourself, or something you can pay a specialist to do, depending upon the amount of time you are prepared to spend on social media, your internet skills and your marketing budget. We'll look at what you can do yourself first.

Arranging for automatic web searches on mentions of your business is a good starting point. The major search engines provide alert services that deliver regular search reports on search terms; for example Yahoo! Alerts (http://beta.alerts.yahoo.com/main.php?view=create_news_step1) and Google Alerts (http://www.google.com/alerts). All these type of alert services allow the reports to be delivered using email; some also allow delivery by text message and as a newsfeed on your RSS reader. These searches will pick up on content on websites, blogs, open wikis and other publicly available parts of the web.

Second, if you have set up a blog, your blogging platform may provide a means for tracking comments that link back to your blog. Regular use of such a tracking facility will help you identify negative comments.

Third, search on industry-specific websites to pick up on comments about your business. The chatrooms of some sites are so active that content may appear and then disappear again before the search engines skim over and record the comments about your business. For these sites, the damage of such comments is arguably minimal because they appear for so short a time. It is the sites where comments remain online for more than a few days that arguably cause the most damage.

If you want your monitoring activities to be more detailed than search engine alerts, this can become a time-consuming task. To cater for those that don't have the time or skills to effectively monitor what's being said about their businesses on the web, a number of services have sprung up that, for a fee, will do all the hard work for you. Service providers can provide a variety of different types of reports, typically including:

- all comments about your business online within a certain period;

- analysis of these comments.

Examples of companies providing these services are Brandseye (http://www. brandseye.com) and Market Sentinel (http://www.marketsentinel.com).

BUILDING ON YOUR REPUTATION

In this section, the approaches to managing reputation are largely reactive in nature: responding to what's out there already, in one way or another. It is worth emphasizing, however, that the best way of protecting the online reputation of your business is to proactively build on that reputation, rather than simply waiting for others to make positive or negative comments about you. Furthermore, it is easier to successfully react to positive or negative comments if you already have a credible online presence that can be used as part of the means to react.

There are numerous ways of building an online reputation. In Parts 1 and 2, we explored the key types of social media and how to use them for your business. Here, we'll briefly look at the bigger picture of how those types of social media can be used to actively build on or improve business reputation. Whilst many ventures into social media by business and government could be dismissed as fads, our view is that these efforts by and large help organizations connect with their customers.

For example, the UK government has been experimenting in recent years with using social media to get its message across. The Foreign Office in particular is using YouTube, the user-created video website. The Foreign Office has a 'channel' on the site (http://www.youtube.com/user/ukforeignoffice). At the time of writing, the channel had 83 videos, with users having the ability to comment on those videos like any other YouTube video. David Milliband, the UK's Foreign Secretary at the time of writing, has recorded a number of 'video diaries', such as after meeting with an overseas government. Other videos feature Foreign Office workers talking about their roles, and other ministers discussing current issues.

Whilst video clips of government ministers and their minions may seem a bit dull, particularly compared to some of the other videos posted on to YouTube, businesses can learn a lot from the Foreign Office office's efforts with social media. These efforts help give the impression of transparent and accountable government, and may represent a new line of communication between government and citizen. Whether or not these efforts are genuine or a cynical attempt to appear in touch is irrelevant; businesses can replicate the Foreign Office approach to social media to improve their communications with customers and make them be, or at least appear to be, transparent.

Another example is Microsoft. Allowing its employees to blog is one of the ways that the software giant has helped shake off its former image as an unaccountable corporation, giving it a more 'human' feel. Even simply counting the number of employee blogs listed on the Microsoft Communities website (http://www.microsoft.com/communities/default.mspx), there are over 1500 Microsoft employee blogs. In addition, the company fosters discussion between users and employees on specific issues on some 2000 newsgroups (effectively chatrooms) and forums. This use of social media helps give outsiders a window (no pun intended) into Microsoft, and gives an insight into the diverse range of activity within the company and attitudes of its employees. The company also uses webcasts to complement its more traditional PR efforts. Whilst not every business is going to want or expect its employees to be writing company-related blogs, the freedom given by Microsoft to its employees has undoubtedly altered people's perceptions of the company and therefore improved its reputation.

Protecting Your Reputation

If negative comments have been made about your business online, you need to consider how best to deal with those comments. A considered and well-executed response will help repair the damage; a poor response is likely to cause further damage and is therefore worse than no response at all. In this section, we will not be talking about the legal remedies outlined in Chapter 18; our focus is practical measures.

Of course, in situations such as when highly damaging defamatory comments are made about your business, instructing the lawyers may be the most appropriate response. However, most businesses do not have the spare cash to turn to their legal advisers every single time someone makes a negative comment. Second, for most types of negative comment found online – for example, statements of opinion – there is no legal remedy available and (quite rightly) free speech prevails. Third, if you do get the lawyers to send a threatening letter to the writer of the comment, you may well find that the lawyers' letter appears online – letting others judge whether or not your response to the comment is disproportionate. (If your response is proportionate, this is nothing to worry about, simply something to bear in mind.) With legal remedies not available or a last resort, businesses must look to other means of protecting their reputation.

TAKING ACTION

Proactive first steps

As we have already argued, a proactive approach to online reputation is much better than the purely reactive. Rather than think of ways to deal with negative comments after the event, consider what you can do to ensure that positive content about your business is more prominent than the negatives. A key way of doing this is by using search engine optimization (SEO) and key word advertising to give your own message about your business prominent placing in search results, with comments by others appearing much lower in the results. We considered search engine optimization and key-word advertising, as described in Chapter 4.

It is going to prove tricky to get your business high up in the search engine rankings and on to the key word advertising if you have little or no online presence. This is a very good reason for having a website and/or blog in the first place.

With these proactive steps taken, what can you do when the negative or critical comments about your business appear online? There is no correct answer to this question. You may decide not to respond to the comment, on the basis that a response is only like to inflame the situation, leading to further negative comments from the writer and to people picking up on the comments who otherwise wouldn't have ever known about it.

Exercising your right to reply

You may decide that a response to the comment is necessary, to put forward your perspective. If you do this, try to do so in a manner that minimizes the risk that we identified in the previous paragraph – inflaming the situation. This is all a matter of common sense, but we suggest the following:

- If you make your response on the blog/social networking site/wiki that the writer used to make the comment in the first place, bear in mind that the maker of the negative response is probably in control of that site, or at least has as much control as you, and can therefore control the direction of the correspondence, and have the last word.

- If you wish to respond on your blog, the best way to respond may be to not directly refer to the negative comments or maker of the negative comments – this will simply draw unwanted attention to those comments. Instead, blog posts that demonstrate your business's personality or good points will do you more good. The exception to this rule is where the negative comments have already come to the attention of your customer base or the industry or local media; in this situation, you may have to give a response. Your blog offers a good way of doing this, because it allows you to make your response two-way if you wish, allowing conversation with interested readers through comments on the blog post. This allows you to demonstrate you are being open and transparent.

- However you respond, keep a cool head, keep the response professional and avoid it becoming a personal attack on the maker of the negative criticism. If the writer said that your service is poor, or your products bad, demonstrate objectively and amiably why your service or products are good. Don't get sucked in to a 'flame war' of repeated responses; this will not make you look good and will waste your time.

Removing negative comments

Rather than respond to the comment, you may decide that removing or hiding it is the only option. If a comment is defamatory, and is placed on a website or social media platform owned by a third part, such as Amazon (if it's a product) or Facebook, another option is to ask the website owner to remove the comment. Most site owners will not do this unless you can demonstrate that the comment is defamatory, and so you may have to involve the lawyers after all.

Attempting to get content removed can sometimes backfire. For example, a posting that was placed on Popbitch, the internet site dealing with celebrity gossip, made allegations about David Beckham, the soccer player, in 2002 regarding his behaviour. Beckham instructed a firm of solicitors to get it removed.

The result was that significant attention was given to the allegations and they thus spread into the conventional mainstream media. The issue is: will taking legal action increase the amount of publicity that a negative item about you receives and, if so, is it worth taking the legal action anyway? This all depends upon the fact of the matter and your perception of those facts: do you want to get the negative item removed regardless of the risk of stirring things up further? This is a decision that only you can take; there is no golden answer to the question.

For negative items about well-known people such as Beckham, it must be borne in mind that if they do not take action, they might be seen to have consented or acquiesced to the comment, or verified it. This is a complex area.

Burying negative comments

There is a so-called dark side to SEO; companies that claim to be able to reduce the visibility of negative comments and content on search engines such as Google. Think very carefully before using these kinds of services; they are expensive, not guaranteed to work and just using them could result in damage to your reputation if you are caught out. The web is, quite rightly, dominated by a free speech ethos, and efforts by companies to hide bad publicity are looked down on. These efforts could even result in web users reposting the material you are trying to hide in protest at your actions.

The extreme measure of burying negative comments does raise an important point about these kind of techniques – they can do more harm than good. Unless someone has put online something defamatory or otherwise unlawful about your company, you are probably best advised to live with the comment, and improve your business's reputation through good services or products, and positive online communications using blogs and other social media.

The Legal Context and the Cross With PR

Lawyers have in the past used PR to support their cases; the dilemma is this that lawyers are ultimately concerned with winning the case whereas the PR team is interested in protecting a brand. Marrying the two objectives may be the key to success.

On the individual's side, they need to understand the level of public interest that will arise from their case. Will they be ready for the mud-slinging? What areas of their case or past behaviour are potential weaknesses?

The solicitor and PR Consultant, Sue Stapley has observed:

> It's impossible to bring in communications specialists or lawyers at too early a stage ... The more time you have to prepare properly, the better chance you have of defending reputation and doing a good job. You're aiming to make sure that there are no holes in the evidence that might give rise to communications embarrassments.[4]

---

4   Quoted in R. Carpenter (2004) 'Litigation PR – Dealing with discrimination', Bell Yard Press Press Coverage, http://www.bell-yard.com/bell_yard_press06_.php.

That is the general position, but what about the use of blogs as a means of PR during a legal dispute? This occurred with the Apple/Cisco dispute over the iPhone trade mark in early 2007.

THE IPHONE TRADE MARK DISPUTE

The Apple iPhone was launched in January 2007. Cisco immediately sued Apple for trade mark infringement; Cisco had its own line of internet-enabled iPhones. The company had owned the trade mark on the iPhone name since 2000 after it acquired another company Infogear.

Mark Chandler of Cisco used the company's blog to respond to questions regarding Cisco's legal action with Apple over Cisco's iPhone trade mark. This is the type of language he used to respond to the allegations. Note the plain speaking and lack of legalese:

> *So, I was surprised and disappointed when Apple decided to go ahead and announce their new product with our trade marked name without reaching an agreement. It was essentially the equivalent of 'we're too busy.' Despite being very close to an agreement, we had no substantive communication from Apple after 8pm Monday, including after their launch, when we made clear we expected closure. What were the issues at the table that kept us from an agreement? Was it money? No. Was it a royalty on every Apple phone? No. Was it an exchange for Cisco products or services? No.*

> *Fundamentally we wanted an open approach. We hoped our products could interoperate in the future. In our view, the network provides the basis to make this happen– it provides the foundation of innovation that allows converged devices to deliver the services that consumers want. Our goal was to take that to the next level by facilitating collaboration with Apple. And we wanted to make sure to differentiate the brands in a way that could work for both companies and not confuse people, since our products combine both web access and voice telephony. That's it. Openness and clarity.*

Soon after the blog was published, which did see some general support in the web, settlement was reached between the parties. This is not to say that the blog was the key reason why settlement was reached but does show that lawyers at a senior level can use tools such as blogs to support their overall PR efforts.

IT IS ALL ABOUT BALANCE

What is key is that you strike a balance between the use of law and how it could possibly be seen to play a role in a PR setting.

Perhaps the biggest danger facing solicitors is using strong language in order to promote the cause of their clients. Such an approach might not look so good when it is cut and pasted and reproduced within a web environment such as on blogs or chat forums.

This analysis applies with respect to old media but we would argue has even more relevance in an online world. The speed with which bad news can be moved online means that there may be greater importance to use of PR. Matters are more complex because we are dealing with a diffuse media where individuals can influence an online brand. On the internet, allegations can spread quickly and like wildfire. Lawyers really do need to be careful with their correspondence and have in the back of their minds that it could end up online.

Conclusions

Social media can be used to great effect to maintain and enhance both business and personal reputation. However, when confronted with the use by others of social media in a way that damages your reputation, you would be wise to think long and hard about how to react. An overreaction online – such as trying to 'bury' the other person's comments – or the heavy-handed use of legal action could generate more damage than what you suffered in the first place. Often, it might be better to either engage the creator of the damage in online discussion and try to improve the situation through open communication, or deal with whatever problem the other person has been so vocally complaining about online.

In this chapter, we've sought to highlight the main issues and dilemmas in this area, there is no easy-to-use instruction manual that you can follow to succeed in this area. It's a case of trial, error, perseverance and common sense. Good luck.

Index

About the Authors

Alex Newson, Deryck Houghton and Justin Patten: Part 1: Blogs; Part 2: Social Media; Chapter 19: Online Reputation

Chapters 1 and 2 were written collaboratively by Alex Newson, Deryck Houghton and Justin Patten. Alex and Justin also contributed to Chapter 19. All three are commercial lawyers who are interested in and actively use social media to promote their respective practices.

Justin was one of the first UK lawyers to realize the potential of blogging and other types of social media, and set up a blog for his Human Law mediation practice. The Human Law blog was one of the first corporate blogs to be run by a UK lawyer. Alex and Deryck have both played a significant contribution to the success of IMPACT®, a blog operated by law firm Freeth Cartwright LLP.

Mills & Reeve: Chapter 18: The Law of Social Media

The law chapter was written by members of Mills & Reeve's Technology & Commerce Team, authors of the Naked Law blog (http://www.nakedlaw.com), with contributions from Anne Adamson, Nicola Brown, Kevin Calder, Sarah Cole, Mark Fardell, Nicky Kenward, Peter Wainman and Rachel Witt. The authors are solicitors qualified in England and Wales and specialize in advising on IT and e-commerce issues.

Lee Bryant: Part 3: Using Social Media Internally

Lee is the co-founder of Headshift, a social media consultancy with offices in the UK and Australia. He has been playing with words and computers since the age of 10, and has a strong belief in the empowering potential of the internet. He is also a board member of a social enterprise, Involve, and a trustee of the Foundation for Science Technology and Culture.

Colin Samuels: Chapter 19: Online Reputation

Colin Samuels is an American attorney practising as an in-house counsel at a software firm located in California. He has maintained a personal blog, 'Infamy or Praise' (http://infamyorpraise.com), since 2005 and is a well-known legal blogger. He has hosted Blawg Review, the acclaimed weekly online 'carnival' of legal blogging, three times, with each of those posts recognized as 'Blawg Review of the Year' for its respective year of publication.

Acknowledgements

The editors would also like to thank the following people who have commented on various drafts of the book:

- Frances Bell, Senior Lecturer on Information Systems, Salford University, UK.

- Carolyn Elefant, Attorney, Law Offices of Carolyn Elefant, Washington DC, USA.

- Christoph Stroyer, Legal Counsel at the Format Recognition and Protection Association, Germany.

- Nick Holmes, Publishing Consultant in the legal sector, author of the Binarylaw blog, Director of Infolaw (legal information services and publisher), UK.

- Stephen P. Gallagher, Principal of LeadershipCoach, executive coaching consultancy.

- Andrew Mills, Head of Intellectual Property & Litigation, Experian.

The lead editor would also like to thank his wife, Rosie Newson, for her support during this project over the past two years, in spite of the many weekends that it has consumed.